D1757333

returned on
stamped below

25 JAN 2009

ROAD FREIGHT AND PRIVATISATION

Road Freight and Privatisation

The case of Egypt

NABIL ABDEL-FATTAH
Egyptian National Institute of Transport
Cairo

RICHARD GRAY
Institute of Marine Studies
University of Plymouth

SHARON CULLINANE
CREST Consultancy
Hong Kong

Ashgate

Aldershot • Brookfield USA • Singapore • Sydney

Published by
Ashgate Publishing Ltd
Gower House
Croft Road
Aldershot
Hants GU11 3HR
England

Ashgate Publishing Company
Old Post Road
Brookfield
Vermont 05036
USA

British Library Cataloguing in Publication Data
Abdel-Fattah, Nabil
   Road freight and privatisation: the case of Egypt. -
   (Plymouth studies in contemporary shipping)
   1. Trucking - Egypt 2. Privatisation - Egypt
   I. Title
   388.3'24'0962

Library of Congress Catalog Card Number: 99-72848

ISBN 0 7546 1103 5 ✓

Printed and bound by Athenaeum Press, Ltd.,
Gateshead, Tyne & Wear.

Contents

Figures and tables

Acknowledgements

Many people and organisations have provided help in producing this work. In particular, the authors would like to acknowledge the financial support of the British Overseas Development Administration for the original research programme on which this book is based.

Much of the research in Egypt would not have been possible without the invaluable support and advice of Dr Ali El-Mazawy. Onsy Fahim and Georg Fahim must also be thanked for their practical help. The members of the Delphi panel in Egypt from the road freight and associated industries, academia and government provided this work with an Egyptian perspective, without which the work would be less valuable.

Insights into the road freight industry in Hungary were provided by a number of experts, including Professor Balint Heirko, Andrew Bates and Nick Murray.

At the University of Plymouth many colleagues merit consideration. However, special mention should be made of Kevin Cullinane and Michael Roe for academic advice, and Marie Bendell for secretarial support. Any errors or omissions remain, of course, our own.

Nabil Abdel-Fattah, Cairo
Richard Gray, Plymouth
Sharon Cullinane, Hong Kong

1 Introduction

Background

Egypt, together with many other developing countries, has set out on a path towards large-scale privatisation of its industry and commerce as a means to achieving greater economic prosperity. Most of the economy is affected by this development, not least the road freight transport sector. The objectives of this book are to investigate and analyse the structure of the road freight industry in Egypt, and to identify how the privatisation and deregulation of that industry are being approached. It includes a review of the road freight industry's performance, its problems during the transitional period leading to privatisation, and the current and likely future impact of economic reform on the industry. Since there is no single ideal route to privatisation, it also considers different privatisation options. For example, the existing large state sector road freight companies could continue as large-scale private entities, or their assets could be sold to the many small freight operators of the thriving co-operative sector. The book also looks at the impact of foreigners purchasing Egyptian road freight companies, a feasible development in a world of ever-increasing global alliances in international shipping and intermodal transport and a topic of much debate in Egypt.

All such developments are considered in the light of past Egyptian experience, and the lessons to be learnt from the privatisation of road freight in other countries are taken into account. Two countries in particular are considered - the UK and Hungary. There are good reasons for selecting these countries. The UK was one of the first countries in the world to deregulate its road haulage industry, and was also one of the leading countries in the privatisation processes that started in the late 1970s and continue to this day. It has experienced many forms of privatisation, and it also has a well-documented history of road freight privatisation. Hungary has been selected because it has some similarities with Egypt, in that it is also going through the

1

process of privatisation and deregulation, and has a well-established road freight industry. The evidence of this book is supported by the findings of a Delphi study of Egyptian experts, undertaken by the authors, drawn from government, academia and the road freight and associated industries. The results of this study enable the book to include a specific Egyptian viewpoint.

There are three main groups of reader who are likely to have an interest in this book. First, it should have a general appeal to all those interested in the topic of privatisation, particularly its progress in developing countries. There are many paths to privatisation, not all of them successful. This book examines both successes and failures and seeks to adopt a critical approach. The very idea of privatisation has been called into question by some commentators, particularly in the context of transport, which often has prominent environmental and social factors to be taken into account. For this reason this book devotes a chapter to the external environmental or social costs associated with road haulage and its privatisation.

The book can also be seen as part of the increasing body of published work on business logistics and supply chain management. There has been a rapid growth of interest in logistics in recent years as manufacturers, retailers and other members of the supply chain appreciate the benefits of an integrated approach to production, the management of inventory, customer service and transport, particularly when associated with international distribution. The globalisation of international business and its supply chains has led to a world-wide demand for higher quality freight transport services by all transport modes. Most of the literature on logistics is associated with developed countries, particularly in North America and Western Europe, and there is a shortage of published work on logistics in or for developing countries, which are, nevertheless, part of the same global supply system. A chain is as strong as its weakest link, and a supply chain will similarly be no more efficient than its weakest logistics link. Poor transport systems in developing countries reduce the effectiveness of international supply chains and, consequently, the attractiveness of such countries for general industrial investment by overseas corporations.

The area of interest for the third group of readers is linked to the preceding theme. Those with an interest in developments in international shipping are aware of the growth of intermodal transport systems, particularly for containers moving by ocean liner services. Shipping companies can no longer only be interested in the sea journey of the goods and containers they are carrying, if they are to compete effectively. Exporters and importers increasingly require door-to-door services from factory to warehouse and want to undertake 'one-stop shopping', dealing with a single transport operator or logistics provider. It is seldom easy for ocean liner companies to integrate with the land system in developing countries, which often lack adequate road or rail infrastructures or suitable inland transport organisations. Since the road freight carried by the state sector in Egypt is strongly associated with traffic moving through seaports, the book is also a contribution to the international transport literature, specifically the interface between sea and land transport.

Structure of the book

The following six main themes are presented in this book:

- The growth of the private economy.
- Privatisation in Egypt.
- The Egyptian road freight industry.
- Road freight management under privatisation.
- Macroeconomic problems facing privatisation of the road freight industry.
- The external cost of road freight under privatisation.

The growth of the private economy

The removal of central planning from an economy and the transfer of some or all economic activities to the private sector is widely assumed to lead to an increase in the efficiency of the whole economy. The essential argument in favour of private ownership is that it is integral to a market economy, enabling a rapid response to market signals. It is also claimed to provide significant longer-term opportunities for redistribution of wealth and income, although it must be admitted that the most immediate benefit that many governments derive from privatisation is the revenue from sales of state-owned assets. Whether or not privatisation will benefit a developing country such as Egypt in the longer run is still to be determined and, indeed, privatisation may bring its own problems such as increased pollution and other social and environmental costs external to the business undertaking. Nevertheless, the prevailing orthodox view is that increased privatisation will be beneficial to developing countries with a tradition of state ownership.

Privatisation may take many forms and, in particular, the impact of the time-scale of its introduction needs to be considered. For example, there is a so-called 'shock therapy' strategy which applies measures to achieve economic stability *simultaneously with* the privatisation process, as for example in Poland. Such a sudden and severe approach may prove very unsettling to a national economy. In contrast, the 'strategy of gradualism' relies on a package of measures of economic stabilisation *as a precondition* of the introduction of privatisation, as applied in Hungary and Egypt. In the latter case, the immediate social costs of economic reform and privatisation have been less severe than in countries applying the shock therapy approach.

A distinction should also be made between 'spontaneous' privatisation and 'central' privatisation. The former, applied for example in Hungary, is a decentralised process by which the managers and employees of a state-owned enterprise transform the entire enterprise or part of it into a private sector company. The process is usually initiated by the enterprise itself, and the terms of the deal are reached by negotiation with the employees. On the other hand, the approach of Egypt has been to apply centrally-controlled privatisation, which has required the government to allocate responsibility for the privatisation of state enterprises to one or more of its own agencies. This approach means that the government's direct influence is still very strong during the privatisation process.

There are various methods of privatisation, which may be grouped under three headings; public flotation by fixed price offer or sale by tender; direct sale to a third party or by employee buy-out; and sale by vouchers. The voucher method of privatisation, used for example in Poland and Russia, is usually associated with large-scale privatisation applied as 'shock therapy'. The management or employee buy-out is probably more desirable for promoting wider employee share ownership or lower transaction costs. This approach, together with public flotation, tends to be used in the gradual or case-by-case approach applied in Egypt, as well as in the UK and Hungary, although in substantially different ways in each country.

There are problems facing the introduction of privatisation to developing or transitional economies. For example, there is often a lack of domestic savings to finance privatisation, and although this could be overcome by allowing foreign capital to buy state-owned enterprises, the fear may exist of overseas ownership leading to foreign control or backdoor colonialism. The outcome of the privatisation process may be to create its own macroeconomic problems including increased prices, a decline in the real wages of employees, increased unemployment, and inequality of income distribution.

Privatisation in Egypt

The revolution of the 1950s led by President Nasser resulted in the state assuming a central role by introducing a planned economy through the nationalisation of all major businesses. However, by the middle of the 1970s, after Sadat succeeded Nasser as Egypt's president, it had become clear that the Egyptian economy had proved to be inefficient under state ownership, and it was close to collapse for a number of reasons. In order to accelerate economic growth, Egypt started to replace central planning with an increase in market activity in the economy. Termed 'infitah' or 'open door' the more outward looking policy was designed to encourage both domestic and foreign private investment in Egypt. This was attempted through two main operations; first, by liberalising or deregulating the economy, and then by privatisation.

When Egypt started the liberalisation reform programme it was suffering from many economic problems, partly caused by rapid population growth, but also by internal inefficiencies, huge external debts and even misuse of foreign aid. As Harris (1988) put it, the causes of Egypt's economic difficulties include 'bureaucratic inefficiency, poor planning and inappropriate past policies resulting in cost/price distortions which have discouraged productive sectors and exports'. The decade after 1975 tended to conceal these problems because of a degree of prosperity brought about by an oil-related rise in foreign exchange earnings. However, in the second half of the 1980s, when oil prices collapsed, it became clear to many that there was an urgent need to speed up economic reform and pursue a policy of privatisation.

Egypt has adopted a gradualist approach to privatisation in order to minimise the social effects of economic restructuring. However, heavy external debts have reduced the government's ability to accelerate the privatisation programme, despite some relief through foreign banking authorities writing off some of Egypt's official (i.e. government) debts. With the reduction in the budget deficit, price adjustments, an increase in tax revenue, and through cutting subsidies, the Egyptian government has managed to accelerate the privatisation programme since 1993, although in 1996 the state sector still comprised 312 companies. The road freight industry forms an important component of the overall privatisation process because of its pivotal role in delivering goods to and from other industries, particularly international trade through the ports.

The Egyptian road freight industry

Egyptian road freight services became part of the state sector during the 1960s. The exception to this was small firms with less than five vehicles which were combined into associations to become the co-operative sector. By the end of the 1960s there were five large state sector road haulage companies, all mainly concerned with the transport of imports from the ports. In terms of tonnage carried, however, road freight was dominated by the co-operative sector by the beginning of the 1990s. There has also been a limited volume of private sector road haulage, although the distinction between the state and private sector is not always clear-cut.

The state sector companies have suffered during the 1990s for a number of reasons associated with unfair competition brought on by incomplete liberalisation of the transport sector. Subsidised railways and inland water transport companies have been able to offer lower prices. The co-operatives, with low overheads, have undercut the state sector companies, as have the transport departments of manufacturing companies, who traditionally carry only their own goods, but are permitted under deregulation to carry the goods of other companies. The former no longer pay a fee to the state sector companies, and the latter cross-subsidise road freight costs as part of their production costs.

Road freight management under privatisation

Privatisation is a global phenomenon, and it is enlightening to make international comparisons. For example, despite the many economic and socio-cultural differences between the UK and Egypt, it is possible to identify similar patterns and developments, although not necessarily taking place at the same time. In the UK a number of studies from the 1960s to the 1980s discovered that the quality of road freight management was deficient, particularly in the area of accurate or effective costing. However, in more recent times, British road freight or distribution companies have acquired a reputation for efficiency, especially compared with continental European competitors operating under more regulated systems. In Egypt, a recent United Nations report (UN-ESCWA, 1994) described the state sector freight operators as unable to undertake effective costing. In developed economies the customers of road hauliers are adopting a supply chain or logistics approach, taking into account many factors other than freight rates. They seek to obtain the best combination of inventory levels and locations, quality and speed of delivery, and other aspects of customer service. These are required at an affordable price, and although freight transport costs are not the only consideration, they are important. If Egypt is to operate an efficient road freight industry it will require many management skills, but an effective costing system is a prerequisite of effective management, and therefore the book focuses on that issue.

Macroeconomic problems facing privatisation of the road freight industry

The structure of the Egyptian road freight industry is compared with those in the UK and Hungary. They are all similar, in that the sector in each country is highly fragmented with a few large operators and many small operators. However, there are also striking differences. In the UK there is no state or co-operative sector, although there is a history of previously state-owned road haulage. In the UK the hire and reward sector (professional road freight operators) has grown relative to own-account operators (manufacturing or other companies carrying their own goods), although in Egypt the reverse is apparent. One reason for this is the much greater attention paid to quality of service by British road haulage companies in recent years, whereas in Egypt it appears that manufacturers do not trust the quality of the haulage sector and continue to use their own vehicles. Furthermore, manufacturers and retailers in developed economies such as Britain are more inclined to adopt an approach that takes into account a range of logistics factors, and therefore seek 'value-added' facilities in addition to transport, such as warehousing and inventory management.

On the face of it, Egypt and Hungary seem to have a similar recent structure of road freight industry with large state-owned companies in the process of privatisation, and with a thriving co-operative sector. Nevertheless, there are significant differences. For example, the ownership of the co-operatives differs in the two countries. In Egypt, the co-operatives are essentially a collection of small private firms, since the small operators own the capital of the co-operatives. In contrast, in Hungary the co-operatives themselves own the capital. This difference may have implications for the privatisation process, particularly since the co-operative operators in Egypt are seen as a market for the assets (e.g. vehicles) of state sector companies when they are privatised.

The external costs of road freight under privatisation

Efficient control of the internal costs of road freight forms an important part of effective management. Internal costs are those for which the road freight company has direct responsibility, such as for the purchase of vehicles or fuel. However, road freight is also known to generate substantial external costs or *externalities*. Such costs are those imposed on the general public or groups of people not directly associated with the road freight traffic. External costs cover the three broad areas of the environment, the infrastructure of roads, buildings and other facilities, and social factors. External costs are associated with the environmental nuisance of noise and pollution, infrastructure damage caused by vibration and road wear, and a range of restrictions on the quality of human life such as road accidents and congestion. Under privatisation the price mechanism is assumed to achieve the best allocation of resources for participants in the market. However, external costs are not reflected in the market price, and therefore government action is required to internalise the external costs, either by making the market pay directly for externalities or by introducing legislation restricting environmental and social damage. In Egypt, as in many other developing countries, external factors have not been given any priority in the privatisation process. For example, Cairo has very high levels of pollution caused by a variety of factors of which traffic congestion and poor quality vehicles, for both freight and passengers, play a substantial role.

The Delphi study of Egyptian road freight privatisation

At the time of writing, the road freight privatisation process is still ongoing in Egypt. Literature on either the process or the effects is in very short supply. A Delphi study was therefore undertaken to elicit opinions of experts in Egypt to shed some light on these major issues. The Delphi technique is an established social survey approach that allows a group of individuals, usually experts, to give their opinions on a complex problem in a structured way. It has been applied to a broad spectrum of areas ranging from nursing to war games. In the Egyptian road freight study reported here, the objective of the Delphi study was to explore the views of road freight experts sufficiently to obtain their collective viewpoint on significant issues regarding the privatisation of the Egyptian road freight industry. The Delphi approach was considered suitable for Egypt where there is neither a tradition of widespread industry-based research nor a substantial body of published statistics or other reports.

Five main issues of privatisation of the Egyptian road freight industry were identified based on preliminary findings. Each of these themes generated a set of assumptions which, in turn, generated a set of statements, which formed the basis for the Delphi study. The five themes, already considered briefly in this chapter, were the impact of privatisation on the road freight industry; the role of freight management under privatisation; the best method of achieving privatisation; macroeconomic problems facing privatisation of the road freight industry; and the external cost of road freight under privatisation.

Statements were used to formulate the first round Delphi questionnaire. The original English version was reviewed and discussed with various transport experts in Britain and in Egypt and was then translated into Arabic. The choice of the panel members is crucial in a Delphi exercise. Since participants in the Delphi exercise should have an interest in the problem and relevant experience, it was decided that the panel should include the major parties concerned with privatisation of the road freight industry, which are academics, road freight transport operators, and government officials. The panel consisted of 23 members in total. The results of the Delphi study are incorporated into the relevant chapters of this book. A more detailed technical explanation of the Delphi approach can be found in the appendix to the book.

2 The growth of the private economy

Introduction

Following the Second World War and the end of the colonial era, many developing countries attempted to become more industrialised; a process considered at that time to be synonymous with economic development. For many newly-independent countries state ownership seemed necessary to mobilise national resources to achieve development, since there was limited domestic capital and any previous development was usually based on a colonial system. The 1980s marked an end to this era, and indeed saw its reversal. The reasons for this change seem partly due to dissatisfaction with the performance of state-owned enterprises and partly ideological (United Nations, 1992). The inefficiency and low output of nationalised industries has been widely acknowledged (Adam Smith Institute, 1986), and many were arguing that private ownership would provide the incentive to improve cost efficiency (Liu, 1995).

Consequently, privatisation, or the transfer of stated-owned assets to the private sector, became a major world-wide trend. It began in the 1970s in Chile, and gained international prominence with the British government's privatisation programme during the 1980s. The idea of reducing state involvement in industry and commerce is certainly not new, but such a large-scale drive to reverse the intervention of government in the economic life of many countries had not been seen before. Despite misgivings about its impact in some quarters, the global spread of privatisation continues at a fast pace.

Creation of the state sector

The decades before the privatisation era saw the growth of the state sector in many countries. A distinction should be made between a state sector created in developed countries such as the UK, resulting mainly from the nationalisation of existing enterprises, and one created in developing countries such as Egypt (Ramanadham, 1991). In the latter case, the state sector resulted partly from the nationalisation of existing enterprises, but mainly as a product of government support for industrial development (Sabry, 1969). The active role of the state in the economy was justified in some countries, including Egypt, by economic independence, while in some other countries mainly under the influence of the Soviet Union, such as Hungary, it was justified ideologically. As a result, while the private sector continued to play a role in the national economy of Egypt, the state sector took over *all* the major economic activities in Hungary.

Bouin and Michalet (1991) have identified three levels of state involvement for firms or other organisations in developing countries: state dominated, state promoted, and serving a special interest. The economic reasons for state ownership revolve around the issues of natural monopoly, the need for economic planning, the advantages of an economic stabilisation policy through direct industrial intervention, redistribution of income and wealth, and an attempt to achieve maximum output from limited resources (Helm, 1986; Helm, 1989; Lawson, 1994). The state sector may also seek to maximise welfare (Molyneux and Thompson, 1987). In all cases, nationalisation results in changes in the balance of power within the national economy from the private sector to the state, and in particular in decisions on prices and investment (Bos, 1986). The extent of state sector public enterprises may be measured by the proportion of total investment accounted for by the public sector. For example, in Egypt public sector investment accounted for 89.6 per cent of total investment in the manufacturing sector during the period 1969/76 (United Nations Industrial Development Organisation, 1979).

The nationalisation process in developed countries such as the UK took place within an existing market economy, while in other countries, including Egypt, it took place within a centrally planned economy. These different starting points have implications for the privatisation process. In market economies privatisation is generally nothing more than a transfer of ownership from the state sector to the private sector within the same framework of society. In non-market economies, however, privatisation is part of a wider operation of economic reform, which includes replacing a centrally planned economy with a market-orientated economy.

The relationship between ownership and performance

The performance of state-owned enterprises has often been the subject of criticism, usually related to their lack of profitability and efficiency due to ineffective allocation of resources and poor management. Evidence suggests that the productivity of state sector enterprises is generally lower than that of the private sector, although this may not be the fault of the managers of the state enterprises. It is clear that governments have used the state sector to achieve particular social objectives through imposing constraints on the enterprises under their control, and in doing so have added to the total government deficit (Bouin and Michalet, 1991). For example, they may be required to supply goods and services at low prices or maintain over-employment, which may well result in poor productivity in such companies. Furthermore, government priorities may change frequently or be too complex, making it difficult for the management of such enterprises to follow consistent goals (Ferner and Colling, 1991; Ramanadham, 1991).

Whether or not there is a direct relationship between performance and ownership is somewhat debatable, although Mayer (1989) argues that empirical studies show little direct relationship. Yarrow (1986) concludes to the contrary that privatisation has led to improved performance. In a study comparing the performance of two Australian airlines, Davies (1971) found that the private company was more efficient than the state-owned company. In a study of 500 corporations in the USA, of which 419 were private enterprises, 58 state-owned, and 23 mixed enterprises, Boardman and Vining (1989) concluded that both mixed enterprises and state-owned enterprises performed worse than private enterprises.

The essential way in which private ownership operates differently from state ownership is explained by Davies (1971) as the ability of private companies to transfer the ownership or exchange the property rights of the company. Since ownership in the state sector is not transferable, the decision maker is less likely to bear the consequences of any decision, whether beneficial or detrimental, than under private ownership. Therefore the switch to private ownership should also result in improved cost efficiency by sharpening managerial incentives and replacing defective bureaucratic control with a responsive capital market (Liu, 1995). Private ownership relies on incentives provided by the market to encourage technical or productive efficiency within the firm.

The difference in performance between the state sector and private enterprises may be a result of the difference in behaviour between private and state management. The notion of the relationship between ownership and management found its origin in the theory of the firm, where the manager and the shareholders are assumed to share identical objectives. On this basis,

11

privatisation entails the adoption of management objectives that respond to the wishes of the shareholders, which is to maximise profits (Alchain and Demsetz, 1972). However, it has been argued that the separation of ownership and control, characteristic of most larger modern firms, may undermine this assumption. A conflict may arise between the objectives of shareholders and those of employed managers of the firm, since the latter will pursue their own objectives at the expense of maximising shareholders' benefits (Short, 1994). On the other hand, Bouin and Michalet (1991) claim that the threat of bankruptcy or take-over of the firm, the obligation of management to produce results, and the threat of being dismissed are guarantees that private management will fulfil the shareholders' objectives. For Parker (1994), the efficiency of firms lies in the agent-principal relationship between management and ownership, and the key to improved performance is competition. Consequently the largest gains in efficiency are likely to be secured when privatisation is coupled with market liberalisation.

Competition and deregulation

The effect of privatisation, as a means of increasing efficiency, depends to a large extent on the introduction of competition. Competition is often introduced through deregulation, although the degree of competition and the extent of regulation may obscure the effect on the efficiency of private ownership (Liu, 1995). Yarrow (1986) points out that competition and regulation are likely to be more important in determining economic performance than ownership. In their study of the experience of privatisation in ten developing countries, Bouin and Michalet (1991) found that the transfer of ownership rights resulted in improvements in efficiency, but these were limited by the uncertain effect of privatisation on market structure. They concluded that market competition underpins economic efficiency, and is, furthermore, the most important mechanism for maximising consumer benefits and also for limiting monopoly power. Competition leads to efficiency by allowing consumers to purchase from lowest-cost suppliers, and by encouraging firms to minimise production costs (Domberger and Piggott, 1994). Even within the framework of state ownership, there is a difference in performance between firms depending on whether the market is competitive or not (Aylen, 1987).

Deregulation may be seen as the removal of the restrictions on competition in general, and of restrictions on pricing in particular, or the removal of barriers to market entry and exit (Bishop and Kay, 1988; Bamford, 1995). The objective of imposing regulations in the first place is usually to correct existing distortions, which prevent market forces from allocating resources optimally (Guria, 1989). In the transport industry, the reasons for regulation generally concern the role of the state in providing and maintaining a national transport system, which is accessible to all who have need of it (Williamson *et al*, 1983). In the road freight industry, a major reason for regulation would appear to be the fear of competition for the railways (OECD, 1990). Regulations may have two objectives: first, to maintain a certain minimum quality of service, usually known as quality regulation; and, second, to bring stability to situations where competition results in price instability (Williamson *et al*, 1983; Guria, 1989). It includes entry and price controls and restrictions on operating, such as the number of vehicle licenses issued, geographic areas served, route restrictions, types of vehicles used, and types of commodities carried. These regulations are known as quantity (or economic) regulations, and it is usually this type of regulation that deregulation is intended to relax or remove rather than quality regulation.

An argument against economic regulation in the road freight industry is that it results in higher costs for both operators and customers, inefficient management, and inefficient allocation of transport resources. In a study of the road freight industry in the USA, Winston (1985) found that entry and exit regulations raise operators' costs substantially. Also, restrictions on access to routes increase the inefficiency of the industry and raise operating costs (Adrangi *et al*, 1995). Under deregulation it is assumed that freight rates will fall for three reasons. First, the degree of competition is likely to increase by eliminating geographical and pricing restrictions. Second, the removal of entry restrictions should encourage new operators to enter the market, pushing prices down. Third, the removal of restrictions on operating freight vehicles is likely to increase the overall efficiency of the industry, reducing the cost of providing a suitable service and encouraging price reductions (McClave *et al*, 1986). On the other hand, there are arguments against deregulation. Relaxation of regulatory controls may result in a reduced level of service, or even deny essential services to small shippers and communities. Competition may result in large operators competing for business in such a manner as to drive smaller operators from the market (Williamson *et al*, 1985). Free entry and liberalisation of charges could have an adverse effect on safety, although strict regulation of safety aspects can be treated as a separate issue from economic regulation, and safety regulations remain under all types of regulatory systems. Nevertheless, many environmental or social problems may be disregarded under deregulation.

There is evidence that deregulation generally has positive effects on the road freight industry for both operators and customers (OECD, 1990). Under deregulation the efficiency of firms has increased, and rates have generally declined, due to an increase in the number of new entrants into the market, bringing greater competition. The range of services offered has also generally increased. One such example was the deregulation of the interstate road freight industry in the USA (Winston *et al*, 1990). The positive effect of deregulation on costs has caused substantial productivity growth in the industry (Ying, 1990). Nevertheless, the experience in the USA showed that after the deregulation of the interstate road freight industry, the number of bankruptcies rose sharply and there was a substantial fall in prices leading to a reduction in profit margins. These market developments, in fact, were not exclusively due to deregulation, since it took place during a recession and the higher level of bankruptcy was not abnormal according to the Interstate Commerce Commission (Button and Chow, 1983; Baum, 1991). In the UK, the proportion of bankruptcies following deregulation was no higher in transport firms than in other types of business (Baum, 1991).

The most undesirable effect of deregulation seems to be the tendency towards concentration of industry in the absence of a competitive environment. However, there is no evidence of this in the road freight industry, since there would appear to be no significant economies of scale for 'pure' transport operators, and the economic barriers to entry are low (OECD, 1990). Other factors, such as the growth of so-called 'value-added logistics', where logistics providers offer a range of services apart from transport and where there are economies of scale, appear to be squeezing medium-sized companies out of the road haulage industry in developed countries. Large companies are able to offer a portfolio of logistics services and small companies are able to specialise as transport operators, often subcontracted to large companies. This topic is pursued in chapter five in more detail.

In Egypt, the road freight industry is a regulated industry, and is subject to both quality and quantity regulations, where tariffs, imports of goods vehicles, conditions of registering, maximum haulage capacity of registered operators, and the number of goods vehicles to be registered are determined by the Ministry of Transport. Although the regulations concerning price tariffs have not been enforced, the other economic regulations were still in existence in the middle 1990s.

Privatisation

A world-wide phenomenon

During the 1970s, state intervention came to be questioned in both developed and developing countries, particularly its role in the allocation of resources, and in promoting economic welfare (Allsopp, 1989). In developing countries, problems of external debt, budget deficits, and low tax revenue signified the collapse of development based on central planning. Privatisation was proposed for both developed and developing countries as the solution to economic problems, and in many developing countries it required the replacement of central planning with a market-based economy.

The key argument in favour of private ownership is that it is integral to a market economy, where participants respond quickly to market signals (Husain and Sahay, 1992). It has also been claimed that private ownership restores incentives, promoting production efficiency, and allows enterprises to be free from political interference in managerial decision-making (Domberger and Piggott, 1994). However, the most immediate benefit from privatisation for any government is likely to be the revenue from sales of state-owned assets (Mayer, 1989), and this may not necessarily be beneficial to the market process.

Privatisation has been taking place throughout the world. In North America, the USA is a prominent exporter of the concept, and Canada has taken on a substantial privatisation programme. In Central and South America, many countries are following the same route (Letwin, 1988). In Western Europe, the UK was the pioneer but other European countries such as France, Italy, and Germany have also undertaken major privatisation programmes. More dramatic privatisation programmes have been announced in Central and Eastern Europe, where the Czech Republic and Poland have undertaken privatisation of their state sectors, as have parts of the former Soviet Union (United Nations Economic Commission for Europe, 1992). In Asia many countries, including Sri-Lanka, Bangladesh, Thailand, and South Korea, are pursuing privatisation policies.

In Africa, economic reform, including the liberalisation of the economy and privatisation, has been undertaken in many countries (Lloyds Bank, 1988). In Arab and North African countries, steps are being taken towards privatisation. Egypt's neighbour, Jordan, is adopting a gradualist approach and had made little progress by the end of 1995 (Abu Shair, 1997). In contrast, Morocco has adopted a privatisation policy based on the rapid sale of companies and banks (Gazale, 1994). In Egypt, a new public sector law was introduced in 1991 which established holding companies to oversee the activities of various industry groupings among Egypt's approximately 550 state enterprises. In 1991 the state sector in Egypt accounted for 70 per cent of gross fixed investment, 80 per cent of foreign trade and 90 per cent of banking and insurance (Central Bank of Egypt, 1992). These holding companies were empowered to sell off assets, close loss-making divisions, raise additional capital, trade in the financial market, reorder priorities and inject new talent into the boards of state corporations to replace existing management.

15

Definition and objectives of privatisation

According to Wiltshire (1987) there is no universal definition of the concept of privatisation and the word has been used in many different senses. However, he identifies four separate components that may be grouped under the term privatisation:

1   The privatisation of the financing of a service that continues to be produced by the state sector.

2   The privatisation of production or a service that continues to be financed by the state sector.

3   Denationalisation and load-shedding, meaning respectively the selling off of public enterprises and the transfer of state functions to the private sector.

4   Liberalisation, meaning the relaxation of any statutory monopoly or licensing arrangements that prevent private sector firms from entering markets previously supplied exclusively by the state sector.

Clementi (1985) identifies four principal strands in the privatisation policy of the British government:

1   To transfer to private ownership wherever possible.

2   The introduction of competition, known as liberalisation.

3   To eliminate certain functions carried out by the state sector altogether, or to sub-contract them to the private sector where this can be achieved at lower cost.

4   To charge the public for public services currently provided free to the user.

The definition of privatisation as the legal transfer or sale of state-owned or collectively-owned physical and financial assets to private owners may be neither sufficiently comprehensive nor precise (Andreff, 1992). Privatisation may sometimes come about without the transfer or sale of state or collective assets, since the share of private businesses in the economy may increase when new and already established private enterprises grow faster than enterprises in the non-private sector of the economy.   Privatisation also implies that new private owners acquire three decisive rights over assets; namely, to utilise assets, to appropriate any returns from them, and to transfer assets and dispose of property. Owners who cannot enforce all these rights enjoy only 'alleviated economic property'.

Letwin (1988) sums up the objectives of privatisation as the following: to reduce the burdens of the exchequer and the state's budget deficit; to consolidate the social and political grip of capitalism by building up popular capitalism; to make the economy more competitive; to reduce the interference of politics in the working of commerce; to bring workers into widespread share ownership; and to speed up the development of the capital market. Other writers also claim similar objectives associated with economic efficiency and reducing the government's financial deficit (Stevens, 1992; Grosfeld, 1991; Lieberman, 1994).

Many definitions of privatisation in essence state that it is a process of denationalisation and transference of state-owned assets or state-controlled activities to the private sector, leading to a change in the proportion of shares of both state and private sectors in the national economy (Pirie, 1985; Kay and Thompson, 1986; Shackleton, 1984; Haritos, 1987; Dodgson and Topham, 1988).

Privatisation in economies in transition

Particular features associated with developing countries or transitional economies need to be considered when defining privatisation. Clague and Rausser (1992) state that the term 'privatisation' has come to be applied both to the sale of state enterprises to private shareholders in Western economies and to the wholesale transformation of the state enterprise sector in East-Central Europe into private ownership. Although the two situations may share common features, the underlying impact may be substantially different. The former involves transferring the ownership of shares from the government to private hands in an already existing market economy, whereas the latter involves changing the rules of the game for all participants, or creating entirely new institutions suitable for a market economy.

Thus, privatisation in non-market economies, such as Egypt, should be seen within the wider context of economic reform. In contrast with developed countries, privatisation in developing countries is a more complex operation, since it may include the creation of a new economic order. It not only aims at a reduction of the state sector, but also requires a new legal framework and the establishment of necessary agents and institutions. This operation is known as *restructuring reform* and aims to stabilise the economy as a necessary step towards achieving successful privatisation. It includes the liberalisation of prices, the removal of controls on imports, freeing exchange rates, reducing the budget deficit, and cutting subsidies (Myant, 1993). It also includes the introduction of private property rights, the construction of a legal system to support them, and the creation of the necessary financial institutions (Mullineux, 1992).

The intended time-scale of the introduction of privatisation varies substantially from country to country. In fact, a country's privatisation policy may be placed on a continuum ranging from instant 'shock therapy' to a long-term gradual process. The shock therapy strategy requires a stabilisation package *at the same time* as the privatisation process, and has been applied for example in Poland (Myant, 1993). The strategy of gradualism, on the other hand, relies on the introduction of a stabilisation package *as a precondition* of the process of privatisation, and has been applied in Hungary (Mizsei, 1993), and also adopted in Egypt. Intermediate strategies may be termed 'controlled shock' and 'semi-gradualism' (Gomulka, 1994). Advocates of the shock therapy strategy recommend it on the grounds that it speeds up the privatisation process with mass or large scale privatisation. In contrast, the strategy of gradualism, sometimes called traditional or classical privatisation, works on a case-by-case basis.

Despite the importance of a rapid transfer of ownership in enhancing economic efficiency, the gradualist approach has the advantage of avoiding the sometimes substantial social costs of privatisation and economic reform. In Hungary, for example, the economic reform which began in 1968 enabled the country slowly to introduce the institutions of a market economy during the 1980s, which laid the foundation for gradual transition to a market economy (Hare and Revesz, 1992). In Egypt, the liberalisation of the economy took place in the second half of the 1970s, leading to the economic restructuring of the 1980s. In both cases, the social costs of economic reform and privatisation were less severe than in countries applying the shock therapy approach. According to 1994 World Bank data, the average annual growth of GNP per capita during 1980 to 1992 was 0.1 per cent in Poland, less than in Egypt (1.8 per cent) and in Hungary (0.2 per cent). The average annual rate of inflation during the same period was 67.9 per cent in Poland, higher than in Egypt (13.2 per cent) or in Hungary (11.7 per cent).

Countries attempting privatisation may also differ in the source of the direct driving force behind the process. Spontaneous privatisation, applied to some extent in Hungary, is the term given to the decentralised process by which managers and employees of a state-owned enterprise transform all or part of it into a private sector company through negotiation between them and the government (Mizsei, 1992). In contrast, central privatisation, which is the preferred method in Egypt, allocates responsibility of privatising the state enterprises to one or more government agencies.

A variety of methods of privatisation are available and have been applied in countries with transitional economies. In many countries more than one method of privatisation is adopted. These methods may be grouped under three headings; public flotation, vouchers, and direct sale. Public flotation can take two forms; either offering a fixed price for sale or sale by tender on the stock exchange. Direct sale can either be to a third party or through an employee buy-out. The public flotation approach is more suited to larger companies, and requires a well developed financial market, whereas the direct sale approach is more appropriate for companies too small to float, and where the financial market may not respond with a satisfactory price (Bradley and Nejad, 1989).

Privatisation by vouchers is usually associated with mass privatisation and relies on the free distribution of state assets among the population (Mizsei, 1992). Vouchers are certificates distributed to citizens which they may convert into shares in state-owned enterprises through some form of auction (OECD, 1995), a method used for example in Poland and Russia. The vouchers entitle the holder to a share of all state-owned enterprises. They may confer ownership rights directly to an individual or indirectly through a financial intermediary, which in turn has ownership rights in a particular enterprise (Ferguson, 1992). Although voucher schemes have been promoted on the grounds of achieving a form of distributive equity for the general public, and enabling rapid privatisation of a large number of enterprises, they have also been subject to criticism. First, such schemes require substantial government involvement, adding cost and complexity to the process. It is necessary to determine who is eligible to receive vouchers, by whom the vouchers are to be issued, and whether they should be assigned a monetary value (OECD, 1995). Second, the government may suddenly lose revenue from privatised state enterprises, which might threaten economic stability (Bolton and Roland, 1992; Hyclak and King, 1994). Third, there is the risk that most voucher holders sell them immediately for cash, resulting in the collapse of their price (Gomulka, 1994). Because Egypt has adopted a case-by-case approach to privatisation, the voucher technique is not appropriate.

The management or employee buy-out is particularly desirable for promoting wider employee share ownership (Bos and Nett, 1991). It also permits a lower cost of transaction (Bogetic, 1993), and should be effective in improving the performance of firms (Wright *et al*, 1994). This method of privatisation has been applied in Egypt as well as in the UK and Hungary. However, there has been a difference in the experiences of these three countries in terms of risk financing of buy-outs. The National Freight Corporation buy-out in the UK was financed with commercial banks taking the risk. In Hungary, the banks passed part of the risk to the State Central Bank through offering discount rates (Karsai and Wright, 1994). Taking into account that the banks are state-owned establishments, the whole risk in fact was passed to the state. In Egypt, the buy-out schemes are being financed by the state directly, rather than through commercial banks, in return for a repayment from the annual dividends, which implies a reduction in the immediate revenue of any privatised company.

The sale of state-owned loss-making enterprises is not an attractive proposition for private capital, and there is difficulty in selling such enterprises. However, if the losses are due to market regulations, economic reform and deregulation should make them more profitable and more attractive for private capital. If the losses are due to inappropriate management, restructuring these companies is a necessary prerequisite to privatisation to avoid under-estimating their value. Restructuring state-owned enterprises may involve splitting them up to reduce vertical and horizontal integration, restating balance sheets to write off the enterprise debt, and reorganisation of production processes (Carlin and Mayer, 1992). If this process is not undertaken carefully, it may result in large and possibly unnecessary financial losses to the government, a topic of debate in the UK regarding rail privatisation (Harris and Godward, 1997).

Problems of privatisation

Privatisation has been criticised for a number of reasons, above all the underlying idea that performance is necessarily improved by transferring ownership to the private sector and increasing the role of market forces (Wiltshire, 1987). In particular, this criticism may apply to privatised industries where private owners are able to exploit monopoly power (Beesly and Littelchild, 1988).

There are two main problems facing the introduction of privatisation to transitional economies. First, there may be insufficient capital to finance privatisation due to the lack of domestic savings (Filatotchey *et al*, 1992). Second, there is the problem of increased unemployment.

The problem of insufficient capital could be overcome by allowing foreign capital to buy state-owned enterprises, but it is often ruled out on the grounds of protection of strategic industries from foreign control. Nevertheless, foreign companies would be able to offer management skills, marketing and technical support, and capital for modernisation often needed by firms in non-market economies, and the fear of foreign control could be overcome by determining a maximum percentage for capital owned by foreigners in any enterprise. For example, both Egypt and Hungary introduced a law to encourage foreign capital. In 1989, a law on protection of foreign investment passed in Hungary allowed foreigners to take up to 50 per cent of shares in Hungarian companies without any official authorisation, and later this percentage was raised still further (Riecke and Antal, 1993). Also, in 1989, an investment law was passed in Egypt to encourage both domestic and foreign capital by offering some incentives.

The Delphi panel, described in chapter one, disagreed that the lack of available capital is one of the most important problems facing the privatisation process in Egypt, claiming that there is no shortage of local capital necessary to privatise the road freight industry in Egypt. Consequently, the panel disagreed that the problem of a lack of available capital could be avoided by allowing foreign capital to buy the assets of the state sector, particularly road haulage.

The panel agreed that foreign control over the road freight industry could result if foreign capital is allowed to buy state assets in the road freight industry. In this context, panel members made a range of proposals largely protective of Egyptian involvement. There was confidence in the capacity of local capital. If there were to be foreign involvement, it should be as a joint venture. Road freight was considered to be a strategic sector and one proposal was that foreign ownership should be restricted to less than 50 per cent.

The problem of increased unemployment arises from the fact that transitional economies often operate with excess labour, due to the inefficient type of technology used and to fulfil the social objective of full employment. With the transition to a market economy, it would be expected that less labour would be used and the result is often a rapid increase in unemployment (Bleaney, 1994). In Egypt, where there is no unemployment benefit, this problem is likely to have serious implications both politically and socially. The state sector enterprises have over-employment, which makes them less attractive for private capital, since Egyptian labour law does not allow dismissal of employees. So, even with any government attempt to restructure these enterprises before privatisation, the government has to transfer the unwanted employees to other sectors, already suffering from over-employment, or compensate them. However, the government has limited resources for compensation. To solve this problem it has been suggested that use be made of the revenue from the sale of state-owned enterprises to create new jobs, or the companies' shares to encourage voluntary and early retirement.

The potential outcome of the privatisation process may create its own problems. These include increased prices and therefore a decline in the real wages of employees, inequality of income distribution as well as increased unemployment. Privatisation in an economy such as Egypt is normally undertaken in a wider framework of economic reform. Price adjustment and price liberalisation are two components in any structural reform programme, since most of the production in such economies prior to privatisation is subsidised and prices are regulated and controlled by the state. Even imports are subsidised through state controlled exchange rates. Price adjustment under privatisation refers to the reduction and elimination of subsidies, so that the price reflects the real and true cost of production, and the budget deficit is reduced or minimised. Price liberalisation refers to price deregulation and the withdrawal of the state from responsibility for price control. These two processes are likely to result in price increases. Furthermore, following price deregulation the newly privatised enterprises are likely to increase the price of their products in a search for short-term profits and possibly as a response to increased costs of inputs. It would be expected that price increases during the transitional period would exceed the increase in wages and income of some groups of the population leading to a decline in real wages and incomes of households in the short run. According to United Nations data, the average annual growth rate of real earnings per employee 1980-1992 in Egypt was negative at minus 3.6 per cent (United Nations Development Programme, 1996).

It has been claimed that privatisation leads to inequality of income distribution and to concentration of property ownership (Jiyad, 1995). It is understandable that privatisation as a means of transferring the ownership from state to private ownership, combined with the introduction of property rights in former centrally planned economies, will result in a new pattern of income distribution, although this new pattern need not necessarily be extreme. Data provided by the World Bank suggests that the impact of privatisation on income distribution in different countries will vary (World Bank, 1987, 1990, 1994).

3   Privatisation in Egypt

Introduction

The 1950s were a turning point in the recent history of Egypt. The revolution of July 1952 was followed in January 1953 by the dissolution of all political parties and the establishment of a new organisation called the Liberation Rally. In June the monarchy was abolished and the Republic of Egypt established. British troops were withdrawn from the Suez Base in the Canal Zone in October 1954. The new constitution was proclaimed in January 1956, and it was approved by a national plebiscite in June of the same year. It marked the end of a transitional period of government between the fall of the old system and establishment of the new one, and, according to the National Charter, the end of any possibility of a return to the old system. The new revolutionary regime announced the beginning of the social and economic readjustment of Egypt. A nation-building project began to take shape, aimed at industrialisation initiated by the state.

In terms of the economic structure, the intention was to nationalise all major financial, industrial and commercial businesses, whether foreign or Egyptian, to become the foundation of a vast state sector acting as the strategic motor of development (Mahjoub, 1990). The land reform of 9 September 1952 was the first step adopted by the Revolutionary Command Council intended to establish social justice. The Revolutionary Command Council wanted to achieve two main targets by this action. The first was to break down the power of the large landowners who, under the old regime, were the political and economic mainstay of the monarchy. The second was to redirect the land owners' capital into industrial development. Land reform would also expand the demand for domestic industrial products from the peasants with more income to spend on consumer products (Beinin, 1989).

The early economic policy of the revolutionary regime was to encourage private capital to develop the national economy. However, private domestic and foreign capital failed to play their assumed role because of distrust and uncertainty concerning the new regime. Therefore the state became a critical factor in the economic life of society in its attempt to achieve the tasks of developing and modernising the national economy. The first major nationalisation was of the Suez Canal Company in 1956 leading to a short-lived military intervention by the British and French. Before the end of 1957, President Nasser announced that 'Democratic Co-operative Socialism' was to be the path for the national economy. The largely private enterprise system, which had existed before 1952, was systematically transformed into a state-owned sector. This was achieved through nationalisation of foreign assets as well as much of local-owned business such as banks, insurance companies and other larger enterprises. Also in 1957 the government embarked on a new economic policy for a centrally planned economy. Presidential decree No. 78 in 1957, set up the National Planning Commission (later the Ministry of Planning), to formulate the first five year national plan for economic and social development. This took place during the period 1959-60 to 1963-64, as the first part of a ten year national plan. In addition, the Economic Organisation was established to manage foreign and local sequestered assets.

In 1962, the 'Charter for National Action' was introduced as the official version of the revolution. The Charter proclaimed that Egypt was to embark on a course based on the principles of scientific socialism. By 1963, state-ownership had extended to all public utilities, transport including road haulage, larger industries, construction, department stores and hotels. Export-import trade and the selling of major crops were also taken over by the state. Small businesses, most retail trade, residential property (except where sequestrated or confiscated) and much agricultural land were left in private hands (Hopwood, 1982).

Economic reform and privatisation

Liberalisation of the economy

By the beginning of 1970s when Sadat succeeded Nasser as President, a quite different philosophy had been adopted for the Egyptian economy. While not wanting to lose the benefits of socialism and the revolution, the regime attempted to liberalise the economy. This was motivated by an Egyptian economy which appeared to be on the edge of collapse for a number of reasons. First, for political and social purposes the government had been directing the state sector companies to employ more workers than economic efficiency required, which made them inefficient and unprofitable (Lloyds Bank, 1986). Second, Egyptian involvement in the Yemen war had drained its foreign exchange reserves away from development projects. Third, the 1967 war with Israel resulted in the loss of two of the major foreign currency earners; the Suez Canal and the Sinai oil fields. Fourth, after the 1967 war, military expenditure increased dramatically. Finally, the rapid increase in population growth and the use of unrealistically high official currency exchange rates had swollen the government system of subsidies.

After the October 1973 war with Israel, and the new environment that it created, a fresh economic strategy was introduced with the aim of accelerating economic growth and modernising society. The socialist and centrist policies were reversed by an 'open door' policy, with stress on the need for an effective state sector and the importance of a private sector working within the framework of the National Development Plan. The reversal was exemplified by the introduction of Law No. 43 in 1974, which encouraged private domestic and foreign investments in the economy (Lloyds Bank, 1986). Egypt moved from being a tightly controlled economy to a more open one. Law No. 43 provided investment incentives, including guarantees against expropriation and nationalisation, five year exemptions from tax on profits, exemption from some import duties, and allowances for repatriation of capital over a number of years. The government started to adjust the exchange rate, by setting up 'the parallel exchange rate', which was more realistic than the old official one. Also, a number of 'free zones' were to be established, where companies could bring in components and materials to be manufactured into goods for re-export and could establish warehouses and other support facilities. The relaxation of investment regulations attracted large-scale investments from Saudi Arabia and the Gulf States, then from the United States and Western Europe. The hope was that such investments would finance new industries that would utilise Egyptian raw materials, supply consumer goods for domestic use and exports and employ Egyptian workers, but conditions in Egypt and in the Middle East as a whole have countered some of these hopes.

Gillespie and Stoever (1988) suggest the following reasons for the poor foreign response to Egypt's open door policy. First, there was a shortage of certain skills due to workers' migration to a number of Arab countries. Second, the infrastructure (i.e. telecommunications, water, electricity, gas, sewage and transport) was becoming overburdened and subject to frequent breakdowns. Third, there was overcrowding and land shortage in and near the major cities. Gillespie and Stoever (1988) also mention a 1979 study carried out by the Economic Studies Unit at the Ministry of Economy, Foreign Trade and Economic Co-operation on investment policies. It highlights the difficulties that investors had in finding suitable locations for their factories, and in negotiating joint venture agreements between foreign companies and state sector enterprises, because of the 'very different mindsets of the private and public corporation culture' (Gillespie and Stoever, 1988, p.29). Instead of supporting new industries, Arab investments were particularly attracted to financial activities, luxury construction, hotels and tourism, and consumerism. At the same time, many Egyptian manufacturers shifted their activities to the free zones to avoid taxation (Held, 1989). A minimal contribution to economic growth rates during the 1970s had been made by Arab and foreign investments, but a higher proportion was based principally on rising oil prices, emigrant remittances and supported by Suez Canal dues (Euromoney, 1990).

Table 3.1
Employment, investment and local income (Egypt 1986/87)

	Employment (Thousands)		Investment[a]		Local Income[a]	
	No.	%	LE millions	%	LE millions	%
Agriculture	4446.7	36.3	9,022	10.8	86,400	21.2
Industry	1731.5	14.1	16,228	19.3	69,331	16.9
Petroleum	32.6	0.3	2,521	3.0	16,901	4.1
Electricity	77.1	0.6	5,916	7.0	5,184	1.3
Construction	563.9	4.6	2,003	2.4	19,886	4.9
Transport, Communication & Suez Canal	545.8	4.5	16,992	20.2	37,555	9.2
Trade and Finance	1236.2	10.1	868	1.0	100,453	24.6
Buildings	208.6	1.7	15,598	18.6	8,200	2.1
Public Services	74.6	0.6	7,712	9.2	b	
Other Services	3338.5	27.2	7,060	8.4	64,411	15.8
Total	**12255.5**	**100**	**83,920**	**100**	**408,321**	**100**

[a] Investments and local income in local currency LE (millions).
[b] Combined with construction.
Source: Statistical Year Book, 1991, Cairo CAPMAS, 1992

Egypt entered the 1980s facing a huge challenge to its economic and social policy. Although the economy had benefited significantly from the 'open door' policy in terms of growth, it had become heavily dependent on foreign aid, as well as on oil exports, Suez Canal dues and workers' remittances. When foreign exchange earnings began to fall off, in particular after the oil price collapse of 1986, the government found itself in serious financial difficulties (Kent, 1993). Foreign exchange earnings from Egypt's staple sources (oil, Suez Canal dues, and remittances) fell by 6.3 per cent in 1987 (McDougall, 1988). Foreign debt put Egypt in the front rank of Third World debtor nations, and its debt-service ratio (obligations on debt as a percentage of export earnings) was one of the highest among all developing countries. Government expenditure had risen faster than revenue, and the state sector had to borrow heavily from domestic banks to finance its deficits (Lloyds Bank, 1986). Another element adding more pressure to the economy was the rapid increase in imports, which jumped from US $4.7 billion in 1975 to US $9.0 billion in 1980 and remained steady at this level until 1985/86. This was a result of a rapid increase in local consumption combined with artificially low exchange rates (Carr, 1990).

Meanwhile, the subsidy system became a major budgetary item, and in 1983/84 subsidies cost the government LE 2,055 million. In that year the inflation rate was 17.1 per cent and the debt-service ratio was 15.8 per cent (Middle East Review, 1986). By the mid 1980s, the government started a programme of economic adjustment to overcome these problems. The first step was the introduction by the government of a new exchange rate system in January 1985, when exchange rates became dependent on market forces. The budget for 1985-86 proposed cutting its gross and net deficit, the latter by a full 25 per cent, to be achieved partly by increasing revenues by 16 per cent with the state sector surplus rising 33 per cent, and partly by limiting growth in expenditure to just under 9 per cent. Subsidies were scheduled to stay at almost exactly the same level (Middle East Review, 1986).

Data for the year 1986/87 shown in Table 3.1 reflects the economic structure as a result of the five-year plan up to 1986/87, and also describes the economic structure immediately before privatisation. The agricultural sector remained the major economic sector, accounting for over one-fifth of local income and employing nearly two-fifths of the labour force.

The privatisation process

By 1987, a new agreement with the International Monetary Fund was achieved, including a package of measures designed to reform the economy (Laurie, 1989). With this agreement the Egyptian government started to apply its reform programme with reform of interest rates and a further cut in subsidies and the budget deficit. The government began talking about the need to privatise some of the state sector enterprises. According to Kent (1993), the aim of this reform programme was to create a decentralised, market orientated economy. The programme was designed to:

- Encourage private sector activity.
- Reduce the state sector size through privatisation.
- End control over investment and eliminate most tariffs on imports.
- Sell manufactures at market prices.
- Raise energy and transport prices to realistic levels.
- Reduce consumer subsidies and target them towards the poorest groups.
- Deregulate private investment.

In the prevailing economic and legislative atmosphere, which encouraged the private sector and domestic and foreign investments, the private sector grew rapidly during the 1980s. The number of companies registered at the stock exchange was 529 in 1989 (Central Bank of Egypt, 1990). In December 1989, a new investment Law No. 230 was issued, which included a number of taxation exemptions, such as that from payment of taxes and charges for a period of five years from the first financial year following the commencement of production or activities.

At the same time, the state sector, previously protected during the 1960s, suffered from the new competition and made heavy losses (Central Bank of Egypt, 1992). By the start of 1990s, the Budget deficit was around 20 per cent of the Gross Domestic Product, reserves were just over three weeks of imports, and the debt-service ratio was 46 per cent of export receipts. Foreign interest payments were ten per cent of the Gross Domestic Product, and total external debt was around US $49 billion, of which US $35 billion was official debt (Timewell, 1991). Another round of negotiation with the International Monetary Fund took place in May 1990, which resulted in the International Monetary Fund approving a $372 million stand-by credit facility (Al-Ahram, 1991). Meanwhile, a programme for structural reform was introduced.

The key elements of this programme were:

- Reform of state enterprises and phased privatisation.
- Price liberalisation and deregulation of state industrial and agricultural production.
- Adjustment of energy prices to reach international levels.
- Investment decontrol linked to price and import liberalisation.
- Trade liberalisation (Timewell, 1991).

The Egyptian government met its 17 main creditor governments in Paris and successfully managed to reschedule its foreign debts, with 50 per cent written off, releasing some pressure from the economy. Combined with writing off long term debts to the USA (US $6.7 billion), and the Gulf States (US $7 billion), the government was able to start the structural reform programme (National Bank of Egypt, 1992).

Egypt embarked on a process of privatisation to withdraw from the state sector and sell enterprises, in which the government now considered that it had no business being involved. Three areas were announced to be open to privatisation; government equity in the 300 joint venture companies (with an estimated total capital of US $577 million), the 2,000 small firms owned by the governorates, and 380 non-strategic state sector enterprises (Banker, 1990). Law No. 203 (June 1991) set up holding companies to take over state sector firms, to find a foreign partner or to sell off the enterprises. The immediate objectives of Law No. 203 were to give full autonomy to state sector companies, to promote the conduct of business along market principles and to expose inefficient businesses. The first step towards privatising these companies was the removal of state enterprises from direct ministerial control (Kent V., 1993). The state sector companies, which were formerly responsible to ministries, such as Industry, Housing and New Communities, Electricity, Tourism, and Transport were grouped under 27 holding companies responsible for all the affiliates in a particular sector. Later that year, the government named members of the boards of directors of those holding companies. The main features of Law No. 203 are the following:

- The holding company shall take the form of a joint stock company, and shall be considered as one of the special persons in law.

- Holding companies shall invest their funds through their affiliated companies and may undertake the investment themselves when needed.

- Holding companies shall contribute to the development of the national economy in their field of activity and through their subsidiary companies, within the framework of the public policy of the state.

In October 1991, the executive regulations of 'The Public Businesses Sector Companies Law' were issued by prime ministerial decree. It included the following three main components:

- *The Holding Companies*: this component focuses on the incorporation, the board, the general assembly, and the financial system of the holding company.

- *Companies Affiliated to the Holding Companies*: this component deals with the foundation, the board, the general assembly, and the financial system of affiliated companies.

- *General Provisions*: this component concerns the auditing of holding companies, affiliated companies' accounts and evaluating their performance; control on companies and the rights of access to registers and books; merging and dividing the holding companies and their affiliated companies; and, finally, the conditions and procedures for terminating the service of workers in companies governed by the law, by resignation of the workers or their unfitness medically for service (Official Journal, 1991).

Also, in October 1991, the government merged the foreign exchange rates into one market-determined rate (Lofgren, 1993). The government started its privatisation programme in four selected governorates (Garbia, Monafia, Asyut and Qena), with such enterprises as poultry farms, handicraft and furniture factories and plants for the manufacture of road-building materials.

The government announced that priority would be given to selling off hotels, cinemas, department stores and manufacturers of consumer items such as soft drinks, biscuits and chocolate (Middle East Review, 1992). In June 1992, the government introduced Banking Law No. 37, giving more scope to foreign banks in their operations, and at the same time introducing more liberal foreign trade regulations (National Bank of Egypt, 1993; Kent, 1993). Later in 1992, the government introduced a new law for the capital market and the stock exchange. The Capital Market Authority had already been established back in 1979 together with a stock exchange in both Cairo and Alexandria. Given that one of the key factors in developing a free market economy is a strong and effective capital market, the government introduced the Capital Market Law (Law No. 95) in 1992 (Central Bank of Egypt, 1993). The Capital Market Authority is a regulatory body, and any company wishing to issue a financial instrument is obliged to notify it. Three weeks are allowed to raise any objections. Also, the law allows the issue of nominal and/or bearer shares, and the establishment of special stock markets (Official Journal, 1992).

In 1994, a massive operation to privatise the business sector companies was launched. In August, the Minister of Business Sectors announced that the government intended to help the workers of state sector companies purchase or obtain credit for their own companies' shares. This facility included a reduction in the interest rate from 12 per cent to 8 per cent without deposit and allowing the price of shares purchased to be charged from the annual profits of the workers (Al-Ahram, 1994). By the end of 1994, the Minister of Business Sectors announced that the government had started a financial and technical adjustment programme to restructure some of the loss-making state companies. This was an introductory step towards putting them up for sale (Al-Mossawer, 1994), and a list of 23 state-owned companies to be privatised was announced (Euromoney, 1994).

Private sector performance

Since the procedure to liberalise the national economy started with the launch of the open door policy in 1974, Egypt has tried to convert its centrally planned and controlled economy into a liberal economy, run according to market forces. The ultimate target has been to introduce a market economy through increasing the proportion of shares held by the private sector and by encouraging and promoting both domestic and foreign private capital investment, and by privatising the state-owned sector wherever possible.

More than 20 years have passed since the open door policy was launched and sufficient time has elapsed to raise questions. The government made clear that the aim of its policies was to attract and encourage private capital to play its role in the national economy within the framework of the national development plan. In that respect, data provided by the Ministry of Planning about the five years national plan for social and economic development may be used to give an idea of the share of the private sector in the national economy, and its performance. According to the Ministry of Planning, shares of the private sector in total investment increased from 39 per cent in 1986/87 to 46 per cent in 1991/92, and was estimated to be more than 50 per cent in 1992/93, see Table 3.2. Table 3.3 shows the amount of private investment in some major economic sectors, and its percentage of total investment.

Table 3.2
Private sector investment (Egypt 1986/92)

Years	86/87	87/88	88/89	89/90	90/91	91/92
Percentage	39	37	46	42	43	46

Source: Central Bank of Egypt, *Quarterly Review*, 1993b, 33, 4

31

Table 3.3
Private sector investment in some economic sectors (Egypt 1993)

Sectors	Million LE	%
Agriculture and Land Reclamation	900	36
Industry	3540	95
Petroleum	2664	91
Construction	485	99
Insurance and Finance	627	95
Tourism	718	97
Housing	2800	96

Source: Central Bank of Egypt, *Quarterly Review*, 1993b, 33, 4

The private sector contribution to Gross Domestic Product (GDP), appears to have increased slightly from LE 31522 million (64 per cent) in 1986/87, to LE 39324 million (65 per cent) in 1992/93, (Central Bank of Egypt, 1993b). However, business sector companies have only been classified as a separate private sector since 1992. For accuracy, 1991/92 data should be adopted. According to the Central Bank of Egypt, Gross Domestic Product in 1991/92 was LE 131,057 million, of which the share of the state sector was LE 50,799 million (38.7 per cent), and the private sector was LE 80,258 million (61.3 per cent). In terms of specific sectors, the contribution of private capital to the production of the agricultural sector was the highest, amounting to LE 11405 million (99 per cent of total production of the sector). This was followed by the tourism sector (LE 775 million or 84 per cent), while the lowest contribution was in the industrial sector (LE 5930 million or 55 per cent), see Table 3.4.

Table 3.4
Private sector contribution to the Gross Domestic Product
(Egypt 1991/92)

Sectors	Million LE	%
Agriculture	11405	99
Industry	5930	55
Construction	2420	69
Commerce	8825	83
Finance	592	23
Insurance	12	38
Tourism	775	84

Source: Central Bank of Egypt, *Quarterly Review*, 1993b, 33, 4

The number of employees in the private sector increased from 7.97 million in 1986/87 to 9.35 million in 1991/92. According to the Central Bank of Egypt, the private sector accounted for about 68 per cent of total employees during this period, see Table 3.5.

These findings indicate that, although some progress has been achieved, more is to be expected during the subsequent years when the new laws, such as those concerning the stock market and banking, have an impact. Finally, although there is no officially announced or documented programme for privatisation in Egypt, this chapter helps to highlight the main characteristics of the Egyptian privatisation programme, which could be summarised by the following points:

- A gradual approach to privatisation is being used to reduce any side effects that might be created during the transitional period.

- There has been a change in the economy and business climate leading to the sale of state-owned assets.

- Privatisation has started with profitable enterprises in attractive sectors such as petroleum and tourism.

- There is a technical and financial restructuring of loss-making companies before releasing their shares to the stock market.

- The aim is to create popular capitalism among the workers by encouraging them to buy and own their companies' shares through the provision of some facilities such as low interest credit without deposit.

Table 3.5
Employment (thousands) in the private sector (Egypt 1986/1992)

Years	Total Employees	Private Sector Employees	%
1986/87	11998	7971	66.4
1987/88	12337	8268	67.0
1988/89	12702	8543	67.2
1989/90	13041	8778	67.3
1990/91	13423	9061	67.5
1991/92	13812	9356	67.7

Source: Central Bank of Egypt, *Quarterly Review*, 1993b, 33, 4

Social implications of privatisation

This chapter has shown that the economic policy adopted in Egypt before the 1950s aimed to encourage private capital to develop the national economy. In the 1950s as a result of the failure of private capital to play its assumed role, the state became critical in achieving the task of developing and modernising the national economy, by adopting central planning. Since the mid 1970s, when it became clear that the economy was inefficient under state ownership, and with the aim of accelerating economic growth, Egypt started to replace central planning by a market economy. This was attempted through two main operations; by liberalising the economy, and then by privatising it. At all stages there have of course been social implications.

Egypt started the reform programme surrounded by economic difficulties; rapid population growth, inefficient bureaucracy in the state sector, a large system of subsidies, growing unemployment, budget deficits, imbalance in the current account and balance of trade, and huge external debts. In addition, the government was criticised for misuse of foreign aid. These structural weaknesses were hidden in the decade after 1975 by the rise in foreign exchange earnings, particularly from the rise in oil prices (Abdallah and

Brown, 1988). In the second half of the 1980s, when oil prices collapsed, and remittances decreased (McDougall, 1988), it became clear that there was an urgent need to speed up economic reform and privatisation.

The privatisation programme in Egypt has been characterised by gradualism to minimise the social effects of the restructuring (Euromoney, 1996), and also due to Egypt's political environment (Ajami, 1995). The government's worries about increasing unemployment, underemployment, and inflation are understandable, with an estimated unemployment rate ranging between 15 per cent and 20 per cent, and an inflation rate of about ten per cent in 1994 (Middle East Review, 1996). On the other hand, heavy external debts, amounting to US $50 billion, with a debt-service ratio of 28.5 per cent in 1989 (Africa Review, 1995) reduced the government's ability to accelerate the privatisation programme. Some relief has come through the writing off of debts. Following the Gulf War, the USA and Gulf States wrote off about US $14 billion. Combined with the results of the Paris Club release from debt (15 per cent in July 1991, another 15 per cent in January 1993, and 20 per cent in July 1994) (Timewell, 1991), the total debt obligations have been nearly halved. However, these debt releases apply to official debts, and the new debt profile is largely non-official. Nevertheless, the reduction of the external debt helped to make debt servicing more manageable. With the reduction in the Budget deficit, price adjustments, increase in tax revenue, and lower subsidies, the government has managed to accelerate the privatisation programme since 1993.

Although recent years have shown a serious effort towards economic reform and privatisation, there is still more to be done. Unless economic structural reform to build appropriate institutions is undertaken, dependency on external factors outside Egypt's control will continue and little development will be achieved. Privatisation seems to be the most suitable way to build this institutional capacity in a more efficient way than was apparently possible under state ownership.

Nevertheless, privatisation may bring its own problems and these need to be highlighted. This chapter has shown that the poor performance and inefficiency of state-owned enterprises have led to a belief that private ownership provides the incentive to improve performance and achieve efficiency. Under increased private ownership externalities, or the social and environmental costs *external* to the firm, become an important issue. To date there has been little debate on the impact of privatisation on transport externalities in Egypt and there is a scarcity of published information. Since this is a topic that cannot be ignored in the longer term, chapter seven is devoted to it.

It has already been shown that there are some problems that occur during the introduction of privatisation or that result from it. These problems have been identified as increased prices, increased unemployment, and a sharp inequality in income distribution. Increased prices during the transitional period have serious implications for Egypt, since most of the basic needs of the population are either free of charge, such as education and health care, or subsidised, such as food, energy, medicine and transport. Subsidisation may take the form of direct subsidy through the government's budget, or indirect subsidy through state-controlled exchange rates. Food subsidy, in particular, occupies an important position in the Egyptian economy, since food amounted to 50 per cent of the typical Egyptian household's consumption in 1990 (World Bank, 1990). More pressure on food consumption comes from the demographic fact of high population growth, averaging 2.4 per cent between 1980 and 1992 (World Bank, 1994). It also results from large family size, and a significant portion of the population not being of working age. The labour force in Egypt amounted to 15 million in 1992, or about 27.3 per cent of the total population of 55 million (World Bank, 1994). These factors lead to a high dependency ratio (approximately 3.7), and higher demand for food. Therefore, it would be expected that a high proportion of the population may suffer during the transitional period leading to privatisation. According to the Central Bank of Egypt, subsidies went down from 12.2 per cent of total public expenditure in 1990 (Central Bank of Egypt, 1993b) to 5.9 per cent in 1994 (Central Bank of Egypt, 1995).

A further problem associated with privatisation is the increase in unemployment due to plant closure and a reduced work force required in the privatised enterprises. In Egypt, in particular, the government's policy of granting a job to all graduates results in over-employment in government agencies, a shortage of skilled workers, and consequently an unbalanced labour market. This problem has been made worse by the emigration of skilled workers to the oil-rich Arab countries. Employment in most state sector enterprises in Egypt is quoted as 20 to 25 per cent above actual needs (Todaro, 1994). Unfortunately, there is no appropriate official data available in Egypt about its labour market. However, with privatisation of state-owned enterprises it would be expected that a considerable number of the work force will lose their jobs, resulting in increased unemployment and a call for a large investment to absorb such unwanted workers. This problem presents a challenge to the government in Egypt as well as to its privatisation programme, especially when the estimated average annual rate of growth 1992-2000 for the labour force is 2.7 per cent (World Bank, 1994). The Egyptian Secretary of State for Economic Affairs has announced that the total work force in the state sector enterprises at the end of 1995 amounted to 974,000 and the surplus of unwanted employees was 70,000 (Al-Ahram, 1996). The Egyptian approach to dealing with this problem relies on adopting two mechanisms. The first one is to increase investment to create more new jobs and absorb as many employees as possible. Total investment in Egypt (state sector, co-operatives, and private sector combined) increased by about 30 per cent in 1994 (LE 35,000 million) in comparison to LE 26,861 million in 1992 (National Bank of Egypt, 1995). The second mechanism has been the creation of the 'Social Assistance Fund' in 1991, to include the unemployed of the privatised state sector enterprises. The government and some foreign donors support the fund. The government's contribution to the fund amounted to LE 150 million in 1992, increased to LE 208 million in 1994 (Central Bank of Egypt, 1994). Increased unemployment as a result of privatisation has one particular further dimension in Egypt relating to female employment. As stated above, Egypt has had a high average annual rate of population growth and had a fertility rate of 3.9 in 1992 (United Nations Development Programme, 1996). Evidence suggests a negative relationship between female employment and fertility (Abdel-Fattah, 1988). Therefore, increased female unemployment is likely to result in a higher population growth.

The Delphi panel agreed that increased unemployment is one of the most important problems facing the privatisation of the road freight industry, but disagreed that it could be overcome by employing revenue from selling State sector road haulage companies to encourage new small road haulage businesses. From the point of view of the panel, the revenue should be used to re-pay the companies' debts, and any surplus could be used to encourage small businesses, not necessary in the road freight sector.

A final problem is inequality of income distribution. It is highly likely that privatisation will result in a new pattern of income distribution, but it will not necessarily be an extreme pattern. For example, privatisation in Hungary resulted in a pattern of income distribution different from the pattern in the UK. Since a strategy of gradual privatisation on a case-by-case basis has been adopted in Egypt, it seems reasonable to predict that Egypt will not experience a sharp increase in inequality. However, in the absence of reliable data for previous years, it is difficult to make a firm prediction.

4   Privatisation and the Egyptian road freight industry

Development of the Egyptian road freight sector[1]

Before 1962, when the first step to nationalise the transport sector was taken, all the Egyptian road freight services were run by the private sector. Between 1962 and 1964, various legislation[2] was introduced to nationalise the entire road freight industry with the exception of firms with fewer than five vehicles. Five companies came under the road freight state sector, four of them specifically for road haulage and one for road building. During the 1960s further restructuring of the state sector took place, when the road building company came under the control of the General Authority for Roads and Bridges in 1966. In the same year two new road haulage companies were established and then merged one year later. Thus, by the end of the 1960s there were five state road haulage companies, all mainly concerned with transporting imports from ports (Ministry of Transport, 1993). They were:

- The General Nile Company for Inland Transport (serving Alexandria and Dikheila)
- The General Nile Company for Heavy Transport (serving Damietta)
- The General Nile Company for Transport Businesses (serving Port Said)
- The General Nile Company for Goods Transport (serving Suez and Adabia)
- The General Nile Company for Direct Transport (serving Safaga).

At the same time, the freight transport operators excluded from nationalisation were assembled into associations, within a co-operative sector.

---

[1] This chapter is largely based on a previous publication by the authors. Reprinted from *Journal of Transport Geography*, Vol. 6, No. 1, Gray, R., Fattah, N. A. and Cullinane, S., 'Road freight privatisation in Egypt: is big beautiful?', pp. 33-41, Copyright (1998), with permission from Elsevier Science.
[2] Law no. 117 in 1962; Laws nos. 77, 78 and 151 in 1963; Law no. 140 in 1964.

The idea was to gather small and individual operators under a single, more efficient organisation, able to tender for business with the advantages of a large fleet. Egypt is divided into 26 governorates or regional governments with one freight transport association established for each governorate, with the exception of South Sinai. The first six associations established in 1964 were in the more populous or more industrial governorates including Cairo, Alexandria and Port Said. In 1996 there were 25 co-operative associations running their own services. A minimum of 11 operators is required to establish an association, irrespective of the number of vehicles owned by each. The association obtains contracts to carry goods and then distributes the work amongst the members, according to the capacity of their fleets. It also collects the revenue with a percentage reserved to cover administration costs and the rest going to the operators. The associations provide many facilities for members, such as buying tyres, batteries and spare parts with interest-free credit.

In 1974, with the liberalisation of the economy, legislation was introduced to encourage private domestic and foreign investment, and the following private companies came into existence:

- The Egyptian American Company for Freight Transport
- The Ismailia National Company for Freight Transport
- The Port Said National Company for Freight Transport.

The exact nature of these companies is discussed later.

As part of the general privatisation process, holding companies were established in 1991 to take over state sector companies as a step towards full privatisation. The Holding Company for Inland and River Transport took over the state sector transport companies, both freight and passenger, including the five state road freight companies mentioned above.

In 1993, the Egyptian cabinet[3] decided to re-structure the holding companies to take advantage of mixed portfolios and to spread losses made by companies over more than one holding company. This was linked with a conscious effort by the government to associate the state road haulage sector more directly with domestic transport. The outcome of this development was an exchange of some state-owned operating companies between the Holding Company for Inland and River Transport and the Holding Company for Maritime Transport, with the former changing its name to Egyptian Holding Company for Transport, Services and Trade to reflect the nature of the new type of traffic.

---

[3] Cabinet Decree no. 217 of 1993.

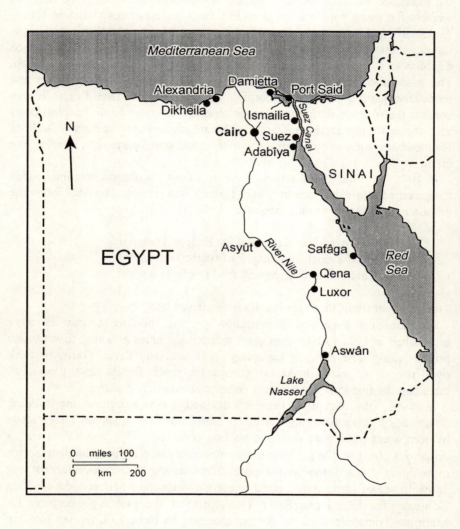

Figure 4.1   Map of Egypt

The Egyptian road network

The Egyptian road network comes under the responsibility of two authorities, the national General Authority for Roads and Bridges, which is responsible for principal roads, and the Local Authority of the Governorates, which is responsible for the roads within the area of each governorate (excluding principal roads). According to data provided by the General Authority for Roads and Bridges (1994), the total road length in Egypt in 1992 was 47,387 km. Of these, 18,327 km of principal roads were under the responsibility of the General Authority for Roads and Bridges, and 29,060 km (including 12,854 km of desert roads) under the responsibility of the Local Authority of the Governorates. According to the World Bank (1994) 39 per cent of paved roads in Egypt were in good condition in 1988. This is similar to the average (41 per cent) of low-income economies.

Size of the Egyptian road haulage industry

In 1992 total goods lifted by all modes by professional operators amounted to 49.1 million tonnes, with road freight the dominant mode (73.1 per cent), see Table 4.1. The co-operative sector dominates the market for road freight transport with, in 1992, 70.2 per cent of total goods lifted (Table 4.2). It can also be seen that the private non-co-operative sector forms a negligible proportion of the total market (2 per cent).

Table 4.1
Goods lifted by all modes in Egypt (1992)

	Million Tonnes	Percentage (%)
Road	35.9	73.1
Rail	10.9	22.2
Water	2.3	4.7
Total	**49.1**	**100.0**

Source: Egyptian Railways Authority (1993), Holding Company for Transport

There is no data available for goods moved (tonnes/km) by the private sector. However, 2.5 billion tonnes/km were moved in 1992 by road haulage operators in the state sector (Holding Company for Transport, Annual Report 1993). By using the average length of haul for state sector operators (which was 246 km), a reasonable estimate of the total goods moved in 1992 by hire and reward operators is 10.5 billion tonnes/km.

Equivalent published data about own account operators is not available. Own account operators are companies such as manufacturers that carry their own goods in their own vehicles. This sector includes state sector production and construction companies, government ministries, and private firms. State sector production companies include the Steel and Iron Company, which relies on other operators for transporting its raw materials and products, but has its own fleet for use within its plants. Other state sector production companies, which rely entirely on their own fleets, are concerned with flour milling and petroleum. Of the eight state-owned cement companies, only two do not have their own transport fleet, although the other six carry only about one third of their products (but all of their raw materials). State sector construction companies, such as Arab Contractors and El-Nassr for Constructions, rely entirely on their own fleets, including vehicles to transport heavy equipment. Private sector companies such as Coca-Cola use their own fleets to transport raw materials and to distribute products.

Table 4.2
Goods lifted by road by ownership category in Egypt (1992)

	Million Tonnes	Percentages (%)
State Sector	10.0	27.8
Co-operative Sector	25.2	70.2
Private Sector	0.7	2.0
Total	**35.9**	**100.0**

Source: Holding Company for Transport (1993)

A study undertaken by international consultants estimated that in 1989 the state sector own account operators had 37 per cent of total national haulage capacity and the private sector own account operators had 25 per cent. It was estimated that the state sector share of the combined national own account and hire and reward tonnage in 1989 was 44 per cent. The private sector share was 26 per cent (overwhelmingly own account) and the co-operative share was 30 per cent (Study of the National Transport System in Egypt, 1993, unpublished).

Road haulage operators

The Egyptian road haulage industry can be divided into state sector, co-operative sector and private sector operators. Each of these sectors is considered in turn.

State sector operators

Between 1985/86 and 1991/92 the quantity of goods lifted by the state sector fleet decreased by 13.8 per cent. During that period the General Nile Company for Direct Transport and the General Nile Company for Goods Transport carried more than half of the total tonnes lifted by state sector operators. El-Mazawy and Lashin (1994) suggest the following reasons for the decrease in the amount of goods lifted by state sector road freight companies:

1 Deregulation of foreign trade, especially imports of foods and wheat, which was previously a monopoly under the Ministry of Supply (the General Authority for Food).

2 Deregulation of cement distribution, which was previously a monopoly under the Office of Cement Distribution.

3 Reform of the Agriculture Bank, which previously had the monopoly of agricultural inputs and outputs.

As a result of these changes, the state road haulage companies lost huge long-term contracts. According to data provided by the State Sector Information Centre (1995), between 1990/91 and 1992/93, the amount of food supply carried by the state sector road haulage companies decreased from 4,587 thousand tonnes to 2,566 thousand tonnes. Also, the amount of fertiliser carried by them decreased from 769 thousand tonnes to 296 thousand tonnes.

The state sector hire and reward hauliers moved an estimated 24 per cent of goods in 1991/1992, an increase of 3.7 per cent from 1985/1986. Tables 4.3 and 4.4 show the proportion of goods lifted and moved by the state sector companies during that period.

Table 4.3
Goods lifted by the state sector fleet in Egypt (1985/86-1991/92)

	1985/86		1988/89		1991/92	
	Tonnes million	%	Tonnes million	%	Tonnes million	%
Direct Transport Company	2.9	25.0	2.7	22.1	3.3	33.0
Goods Transport Company	3.1	26.7	3.6	29.5	2.1	21.0
Transport Businesses Company	2.5	21.6	2.3	18.9	1.4	14.0
Heavy Transport Company	1.4	12.0	1.6	13.1	1.6	16.0
Inland Transport Company	1.4	14.7	2.0	16.4	1.6	16.0
TOTAL	**11.3**	**100**	**12.2**	**100**	**10.0**	**100**

Source: Holding Company for Transport (1993)

During 1985/86-1991/92, the increase in the average length of haul was 20 per cent (from 205 to 246 km), with all state sector companies, except for the General Nile Company for Heavy Transport, recording an increase. This general increase in average length of haul reflects the greater emphasis placed on the transport of international import trade by the state sector companies from the major ports. In 1991/1992 the total kilometres run by all state sector companies was 131.2 million km, of which 32.0 per cent were unladen. Since the main work for the state sector companies is to transport imports from ports, it increases the average length of haul, but it also makes it more difficult to find a load for the return journey.

Table 4.4

Goods moved by the state sector fleet in Egypt (1985/86-1991/92)

	1985/86		1988/89		1991/92	
	Million tonnes/ km	%	Million tonnes/ km	%	Million tonnes/ km	%
Direct Transport Company	547	23.1	675	27.6	732	29.7
Goods Transport Company	460	19.4	528	21.6	452	18.4
Transport Businesses Company	592	24.9	475	19.5	382	15.5
Heavy Transport Company	364	15.3	316	12.9	366	14.9
Inland Transport Company	410	17.3	449	18.4	529	21.5
TOTAL	**2373**	**100**	**2443**	**100**	**2461**	**100**

Source: Holding Company for Transport (1993)

The co-operative sector

In the early 1960s a number of co-operatives were set up to gather the small private road freight operators, often operating as individuals and excluded from the nationalisation processes. They acted under one organisation with the objective of establishing a more efficient road freight industry. These co-operatives were at that time supervised by the Ministry of Industry. It subsequently seemed more appropriate to attach them to the Ministry of Transport and in 1964 the co-operatives (seven at that time) were transferred to its control. The Ministry of Transport continued to supervise the co-operatives through its Inland Transport Authority[4] up to the year 1975, when the Inland Transport Authority was abolished[5] and the supervision of the co-operatives was transferred to the Ministry of Local Administration. In 1978, this situation was once more reversed and the co-operatives were returned to the Ministry of Transport. One year later, each co-operative was placed

---

[4] Established by Law no. 96 in 1960, revised by Law no. 3143 in 1964.
[5] Law no. 100 in 1975.

under the supervision of the governorate administration in which it is located.[6] This was still the situation in 1996. The number of changes in the control of the co-operatives during that period no doubt reflects the wider uncertainty within the central government regarding the changing nature of the relationship between the state and industry sectors. The capital of the co-operatives is not owned by the co-operatives as organisations, but privately by the members. Consequently, the co-operative sector in Egypt could be seen as a collection of private small firms with a degree of state support. It is easy to assume that Egypt is directly comparable with other states where the road haulage industry has a significant co-operative sector. However, the nature of co-operatives is not always the same. For example, in Hungary, unlike Egypt, the co-operatives own their capital as entities (Roe, 1992).

Table 4.5
Road freight co-operative sector in Egypt (1987/91)

	1987	1991
Members	12,112	13,110
Vehicles	13,626	15,204
Revenue. (LE millions)	149.17	157.21
Tonnes carried (millions)	23.11	25.14

Source: General Association for Freight Transport (1988)
General Association for Freight Transport (1992)

At present, there is one co-operative located in each of the 25 governorates (with the exception of South Sinai). The total number of members in 1991 was 13,110 owning 15,204 vehicles, of which approximately 70 per cent were in operational condition (General Association for Road Freight Transport, unpublished data, 1992). There are no restrictions for membership except that the capacity of goods vehicles should be at least five tonnes. A Board of Directors is elected for each co-operative from among its members and there is a central committee located in Cairo with the role of overall supervision of the co-operatives. The major clients of the co-operatives are companies affiliated to the Ministry of Supply (cereal, milling industry products, fertilisers, etc.), and annual contracts are negotiated with that ministry. In addition, the co-operatives receive haulage orders from the five state sector

---

[6] Law no. 43 in 1979.

freight transport companies, as well as companies in other production sectors. In 1991 the co-operative sector carried 25.2 million tonnes, earning a total revenue of LE 157 million (Table 4.5). As stated earlier, in 1992 the co-operatives lifted 70.2 per cent of total road freight tonnage, and moved an estimated 60.8 per cent of total road tonnes-kilometres.

The continuing domination of the road freight market by the co-operative sector is a result of two factors. First, there is a new pattern of demand for road freight services, resulting from the deregulation of sectors such as cement distribution. The flexibility in location and vehicle size of the co-operatives gives them an advantage over the state sector companies, which operate centrally. Second, in the current more competitive environment in the road freight market, the co-operative sector is able to offer lower prices than both the state sector and the private sector operators. The small and individual owner-driver operators in the co-operative sector are likely to have lower overheads, fewer employees, lower depreciation costs, and lower maintenance costs since part of the maintenance work is often done by the vehicle owner.

Private sector operators

Three large scale private companies were established in 1974[7] (the Ismailia National Company for Freight Transport; the Port Said National Company for Freight Transport; the Egyptian American Company for Freight Transport). Data relating to these companies is shown in Table 4.6. The number of vehicles in use by the three companies was 205 in 1990, accounting for 75.9 per cent of the total of the companies' fleet of 270 vehicles. There was little difference in the percentage of vehicles in use by each of the companies. The level of fleet usage is no better than the state sector suggesting poor maintenance and management. Total goods lifted by the three companies' fleets in 1991 amounted to 724 thousand tonnes, more than half of this amount (55.9 per cent) carried by the Ismailia National Company. All three companies carry general freight, although the Ismailia National Company has specialised in imported cement and intends to focus on passenger transport for tourists in the Sinai region. The Port Said National Company specialises in container transport. Total revenue for the three companies in 1991 amounted to more than LE 6 million. They lifted two per cent of tonnage and moved 17.1 per cent (of tonnes/kilometres) of the hire and reward sector.

The three companies are designated as private sector companies registered under Law No. 43 of 1974. However, they are not entirely privately owned. For example, about 40 per cent of the Egyptian American Company is owned by three state-owned insurance companies and about 30 per cent by another

---

[7] Investment Law no. 43.

largely state-owned company. The remaining capital is privately owned. At the time of writing it is difficult to see what the role of such companies will be in the privatisation process. In addition to the above three companies, there are known to be small entirely private road haulage companies, but there is no documented data about them. They are at present likely to form a very insignificant proportion of total road freight.

Table 4.6
Large scale private sector operators in Egypt (1991)

	Egyptian American Company	Port Said National Company	Ismailia National Company
Vehicle fleet	120	81	69
Vehicles in use	88	65	52
Goods lifted (tonnes 000)	254	65	405
Revenue (LE 000)	3030	900	2153

Source: Egyptian American Company for Freight Transport (1992)
Port Said National Company for Freight Transport (1992)
Ismailia National Company for Freight Transport (1992)

Potential for privatisation

The road freight industry in Egypt is a fragmented industry, dominated by large numbers of small firms, with a small number of large firms. The co-operative sector dominates the hire and reward road freight market in Egypt, with 70.2 per cent of total goods lifted by road in 1991. This domination is a result of the liberalisation of foreign trade and cement distribution, and reform of the Agriculture Bank, resulting in an increase in the demand for small firm operators rather than large operators. In contrast with some developed countries, such as the United Kingdom, where hire and reward dominates the road freight market, own account operators continue to dominate in Egypt. The Study of the National Transport System in Egypt (1993) estimated that in 1989 about 60 per cent (35 per cent state sector, 25 per cent private sector) of total haulage capacity was carried by own account operators.

As discussed in the last chapter, several options exist for the privatisation of the state sector road freight companies in Egypt. One approach would be to dissolve them and sell off their assets to a wide number of bidders. The result would probably be an increase in the number of small operators and unemployment would also increase. The experience in the United Kingdom and other developed countries since the 1980s points towards the development of contract distribution within a logistics framework. This topic is pursued further in the next chapter.

Whatever developments take place, there is a threat of underestimating the real value of the companies, due to poor financial performance, over-employment and an unbalanced financial structure. Furthermore, there is the problem of companies' debt, which accounted for LE 165 million in 1995 (Al-Ahram, 1996). It would therefore appear that these companies need to be restructured before privatisation, particularly in the light of similar problems in Eastern Europe (Carlin and Mayer, 1992).

For the state sector road freight companies in Egypt a number of features may be suitable for a restructuring programme, which would need to take place before privatisation. It may be possible to reduce empty running, which accounted for 32 per cent of total kilometres run in 1992, by re-scheduling routes and cutting unprofitable areas. Running costs could be reduced if a more effective and better-trained management undertook closer monitoring and investigation of the cost elements, identifying areas where cost reduction could be made. Modernisation of the fleet would help to reduce running costs, since 32 per cent of the state sector fleet was over eight years old in 1993. The government should be able to sell off unwanted vehicles, since only 67.5 per cent of the state sector companies' fleet was in use in 1992. Existing small operators in the co-operative sector may be able to expand by purchasing such vehicles, or the sale may attract new private entrepreneurs. The government may also consider writing off some or all the companies' debts to facilitate their privatisation.

In Egypt, road freight has been a regulated industry since 1957. Both quantity and quality regulations are applied. Although there are no route restrictions, the regulations include restrictions on the number of goods vehicles to be licensed, the import of goods vehicles, and prices. The stipulations regarding price control included in the law in Egypt are not enforced, but the price tariff announced by the state sector companies requires the approval of the Ministry of Transport. With the privatisation process, and the transfer to a market economy, it would be necessary to deregulate the road freight industry in Egypt by removing economic regulations to allow the introduction of competition. Privatisation of the state-owned companies should go hand-in-hand with changes in the co-operative sector. Better-managed co-operative operators should be able to expand within a privatised sector, possibly purchasing superfluous equipment from the state sector. At the same time, other less successful co-operative operators may leave the industry, also leaving room for expansion.

The Delphi study results

The panel of 23 Egyptian experts was asked to provide their opinions on the impact of privatisation on the road freight industry in terms of performance of the industry, introduction of competition, customer benefits, public expenditure, size of the state sector, and the need for a legal distinction between own account and professional operators. The panel was generally in favour of privatisation, agreeing that it will inevitably create a more efficient, flexible and dynamic road freight industry, and that competition is the most important element for a high quality road freight industry. It also agreed that road freight customers will benefit from privatising the industry in terms of a better quality of service, and that privatisation would lead to lower prices.

However, there was uncertainty about the level of competition and whether it should be regulated. The panel did not accept that the road haulage industry should regulate itself, but there were mixed views about the role of government regulation. The impression formed by this result is that Egyptians still want government involvement, even under a privatised system. Earlier chapters have shown how the privatisation process is more centrally controlled in Egypt than in many other countries. This approach reflects a lack of faith in the quality of business management, which may prove to be a serious problem if new approaches to freight transport, such as an integrated logistics system, are to be introduced. This the subject of the next chapter.

This chapter has outlined the structure of the road freight industry in Egypt and has shown how it has changed over the years with the different economic regimes. It has highlighted the fact that even before the open door policy, there was a healthy private sector which operated under the co-operatives. There were also several large-scale private sector operators working alongside the state sector companies. The existence of the private sector element should serve to make the privatisation process easier in many respects, as precedent already exists. However, as little data exists about the private sector, it is difficult to judge its level of efficiency or use it as a role model for privatisation. Therefore, a more general review of road freight management efficiency is necessary and is the subject of the next chapter.

5 Road freight management under privatisation

Introduction

Privatisation is intended to bring about substantial changes in the way in which an industry operates. This chapter and the following chapter six examine the actual and potential impact of privatisation on the road freight industry, particularly in the UK and Hungary, and discuss whether there are any lessons for the Egyptian road haulage industry. The two chapters approach the subject at different levels. In this chapter the subject is treated at the *microeconomic* level, or at the level of the firm and its management, whereas chapter six looks at road freight issues at the *macroeconomic* or national economy level. It is essential to look at both levels to gain an understanding of the nature and future of the road freight industry.

The focus of the current chapter is on areas likely to be affected by privatisation - operating efficiency, opportunities for change and new methods of conducting road freight operations. Privatisation is intended to improve the efficiency of firms, particularly through an increased awareness of costs. Therefore, much of this chapter is devoted to road freight costing. An inadequate knowledge of costing has been a problem of the road freight industry, even in developed countries, and partly accounts for the high bankruptcy level in the sector in the UK. The major opportunity for change in road freight operations in recent years has been as part of an integrated logistics service. The application of logistics concepts requires firms to balance a number of factors such as inventory levels and quality of customer service. Transport plays an important role in such 'trade-offs', but should not be considered in isolation. Indeed, many firms traditionally operating as road freight companies are now reinventing themselves as 'logistics providers'. This development has implications for Egypt, not only for its domestic internal road freight, but also for its role as part of the global network of trade, including its links with ports and maritime transport. Intermodalism, or the use of fully integrated transport systems, particularly between land and sea using containers, is well-established between developed countries but often fails in developing countries through lack of a sufficient port or inland infrastructure or transport service, including road freight. If Egypt is to prosper in the world economy it will require a road freight system fully integrated with international shipping services.

Efficiency in road freight operations

The ultimate objective of private businesses is to create and increase their profits, either through increasing sales or by reducing costs. It is seldom easy to increase sales since the limitations of the market and competitive conditions must be faced. Money will be needed to fund marketing and promotion, and elasticity of demand for the product must be taken into account. For these reasons reducing costs is often a more direct way to increase profits than attempting to increase sales.

Costs play a major role in transport decision-making for all carriers. They need to know the exact cost of operations to make pricing and investment decisions, and costing is the tool that provides essential information upon which they can base their operating decisions. This information includes, for example, what rates to charge, what vehicles to purchase, and when to replace the vehicles. If any operation is not costed either before or after it is carried out, there is no way of knowing what price to charge, other than observing the prices of competitors. Carriers will also not know whether the revenue received was sufficient to cover all their operating costs and, at the same time, whether they have allowed an additional amount for profit.

There is little published research into road haulage costing, even in developed countries with a strong business research tradition such as the UK. This is not surprising since most institutions prefer to keep the details of costing confidential. Nevertheless, it is a topic that should not be ignored in any discussion of the privatisation process. This chapter therefore considers the nature of road haulage costing, about which there is a reasonably extensive literature, in contrast to the paucity of literature on the actual cost efficiency of road haulage companies. The chapter also draws some parallels between road freight costing in the UK and in Egypt.

Before and during the 1980s the UK road freight industry was relatively inefficient (Hallett and Gray, 1987) with the bankruptcy rate of hire and reward road haulage companies second only to that of building contractors (Key Note, 1984). However, by the middle of the 1990s a later edition of the same publication (Key Note, 1996) claimed that British hauliers were generally considered much more efficient than equivalent continental

European hauliers. Various factors account for this favourable development, and the chapter will examine their implications for Egypt. It will also consider some other features that provide evidence of the degree of road haulage efficiency in Egypt. These refer to the age and maintenance of vehicles, the extent to which vehicles travel empty, and the professional qualifications of road haulage management. Any discussion of road haulage efficiency also needs to compare the performance of hire and reward road hauliers, carrying the goods of other companies, with companies such as manufacturers who predominantly carry only their own goods (own account operators). Again, it is useful to draw parallel conclusions about Egypt and the UK.

Types of costs

This chapter restricts itself to discussion of *internal* costs incurred by road freight operators, whereas chapter seven will consider the issue of *external* social or environmental costs. Internal costs can be classified in a variety of ways depending on the purposes for which the information is intended. For example, costs may change as the level or volume of production or business activity changes. Variable costs change directly and proportionately with changes in volume, whereas fixed costs do not change. Semi-variable costs change in the same direction as, but less than proportionately with, changes in volume. Another approach to costing is to divide the various items of cost into the two categories of direct and indirect costs when calculating the full, or total, cost. A direct cost is specifically traceable to, or directly caused by, a particular activity, whereas an indirect cost is not.

Hussey (1989) describes a further category of costs 'by nature'. The basic classification of costs according to their nature is into materials, labour and expenses, although these broad categories can be further subdivided. Another distinction may be made between capital costs of fixed assets intended to benefit future activity, and revenue costs incurred in running the business during the current period. Costs may also be allocated to the function to which they relate in production, marketing, distribution and administration (Chan, 1987). There are further classifications of costs, including that of Biggs and Benjamin (1989) who state that the main areas in which costs can be classified are stock valuation, decision-making, and planning and control. Lowe (1983) states that there are many sorts of cost under the four main headings of historical costs, replacement costs, standard costs, and marginal costs.

These examples are from just a small sample of the extensive literature on the nature of costs, a full review of which is beyond the scope of this work. In summary, the type of cost classification used depends on the objectives of management, but the more general types of internal costs may be seen as relating to:

- Changes in the level of activity or volume (variable, fixed, semi-variable and semi-fixed costs).

- The nature of the cost (materials, labour and expenses costs).

- Business functions (production, marketing, distribution and administration costs).

- Financial convention (capital and revenue costs).

- The cost objective or activity (direct and indirect costs).

- Planning and control (historical, standard, controllable and uncontrollable costs).

Road haulage costs

Road haulage is, of course, no different from any other business activity in terms of the broad classes of costs it incurs, and all of the previously-mentioned types of costs are relevant to the industry. However, as with many other business activities, road haulage has its own special features and terminology and they will be considered in this section.

Capital costs

The capital costs of road haulage can be defined as all expenditure on the purchase or hire of vehicles, buildings, depots and equipment. Business capital is available from many sources for both the short and long term. The choice between these sources of finance depends on many factors such as the financial strategy and planned requirements of the firm, the current and future financial situation, and the purposes and length of time for which finance is needed.

From the point of view of repayment of costs to a lender such as a bank, sources of finance could be short, medium or long term. Puxty and Dodds (1988) define 'short' to be less than three years, but generally less than one year, 'medium' to be three to ten years and 'long' to be over ten years. Short-term finance includes bank finance, bill finance, leasing, hire purchase, and factoring and invoice discounting. For medium and long term finance, there are two primary sources of funds; internal (from the operations of the firm consisting of profits after tax and dividends) and external (creditors and investors). Forms of medium term finance are bank loans, hire purchase and financial and operating leasing. For long term financing, an enterprise may use banks and other financial institutions or it may issue company securities such as equity or preference shares and debentures. Shaw (1991) includes sale and lease back, and foreign currency loans as further long term finance sources. This is a major topic beyond the scope of this book to consider in detail. However, one issue of particular relevance to the road freight industry is whether to own or lease equipment such as vehicles. A further option for own account operators is to let a third party provide the transport.

Overheads

The term *overhead costs* is used to describe collectively all those expenses incurred in running a transport business, or in operating a transport department within a business devoted to other activities for its main source of revenue, which cannot be directly attributed to any individual vehicle. Overheads can be divided into the following categories (Lowe, 1989):

- Management
- Office and administration
- Workshop and stores
- Branch depots
- Sales and publicity
- Auxiliary fleet
- Professional services

These categories can be broken down into the entire individual cost items likely to be incurred under each heading. Overhead costs could be described as 'non-variable' costs, because they cannot readily be attributed to particular items of output and in general must be incurred irrespective of the level of production. In fact, some overheads, such as supervision, are in certain cases only partly invariable. Once output actually rises above a certain level either the present supervisor must work longer hours or an additional supervisor must be appointed. Thus, the expenditure can be regarded as fixed only within certain limits. Other examples are overtime and other premiums paid to staff. On the other hand, some types of expenditure are more clearly fixed; for example, rent and rates (Practical Financial Management, 1987).

The cost of the overhead items may be spread over the transport fleet in proportion to the expected useful life of each vehicle. To apportion the total annual overhead cost between individual vehicles, two methods are possible:

1   A direct and equal division of the total cost between the total number of vehicles in the fleet (where the fleet consists of vehicles of a similar type and capacity).

2   A division of the total cost between total carrying capacity of fleet in terms of tonnage, cubic capacity or litres depending on the type of vehicle operated and multiplied by the capacity of each individual vehicle, where the fleet comprises a variety of vehicle types or carrying capacities (Lowe, 1989).

Operating costs

Operating costs may be described as the costs required to keep the vehicles in a good condition and the costs which are incurred when the vehicles move. The standard terms used in road haulage for the two broad categories of operating costs are *standing costs* and *running costs*.

Standing costs   Certain costs have to be met by goods vehicle operators throughout the life of each vehicle irrespective of the amount of work it does, the distance it runs or the revenue earned. These costs must be met even if the vehicle spends a large proportion of its lifetime standing idle due to the need for excessive repairs or lack of work. These costs are called standing costs or fixed costs (Lowe, 1989). Standing costs are those which within certain limits, such as the fleet size being capable of dealing with the workload imposed, do not vary with the level of activity, but rather with the passage of time (Wilson, 1987). They represent the total cost in providing and maintaining vehicles and will be incurred irrespective of the amount the vehicle is used (Ratcliffe, 1987). They are often computed on a monthly basis.
   The following six elements are normally associated with standing costs:

1   Vehicle licences: Goods vehicles are subject to two forms of licensing, vehicle excise licences and operator's licences. The rate of duty depends on a number of factors, which vary between countries.

2   Vehicle insurance: Premiums for vehicle insurance are charged annually either on an individual price per vehicle or as a blanket cover for the whole fleet, particularly where large numbers of vehicles are operated. Insurance costs included as standing costs are those which are incurred in respect of individual vehicles. All other insurance such as goods in transit, premises and contents cover, life insurance on the proprietor or

directors and insurance in respect of pension schemes are normally dealt with as overheads.

3   Drivers' wages: If one accepts the fact that irrespective of whether the vehicle works or stands the drivers still have to be paid, the drivers' wages should be looked upon as a standing cost item. Additional payments such as overtime may be dealt with as a running cost (see below).

4   Rent and rates: The operator has to provide land for garaging or parking vehicles when they are not being used and the cost of the parking space should be included in the cost of owning and operating the vehicles. Whether the land is owned freehold by the operator or rented, its cost or value should be set against the vehicles using it. Rent and rates for land and buildings occupied as offices, vehicle repair workshops or for warehousing are normally considered as overheads.

5   Interest on capital employed: One of the most expensive items is the cost of borrowing money, either in the form of loans or hire purchase for purchasing capital equipment, or by way of bank overdrafts to maintain levels of working capital. The interest on capital borrowing should be dealt with as a standing cost item.

6   Depreciation of the vehicle: Benson (1992) defines depreciation as a gradual and permanent decrease in the value of an asset (the vehicle in this case). There are many methods to calculate depreciation, the two simpler ones being the straight line or fixed instalment method, and the diminishing or reducing balance (fixed percentage) method.

Running costs Typical running costs are fuel, oil and lubricants, tyres, repair and maintenance, drivers' expenses and overtime payments, and sundries. Fuel, oil and lubricants are the most directly variable of all vehicle operating costs, forming a very high cost item within the total cost of vehicle operation.

Figure 5.1 shows the typical components and elements of internal costs of road haulage.

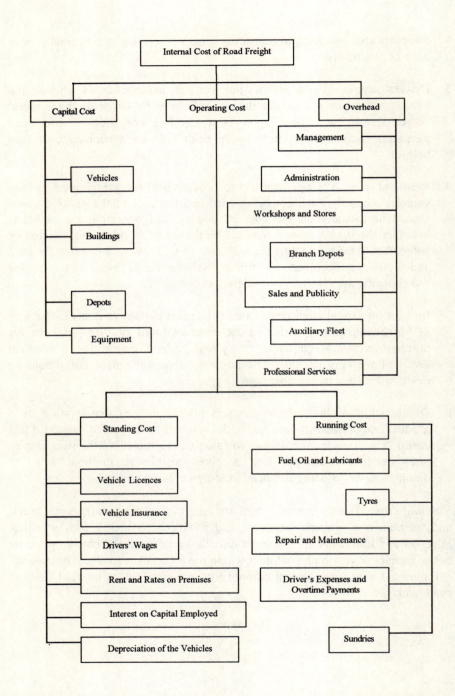

Figure 5.1   Components and elements of internal cost of road freight

Effectiveness of road haulage costing

The approach adopted in this section is to consider the development of road freight efficiency in the UK since the late 1970s and early 1980s as a model for Egypt. Of course, the countries are not directly comparable, but sufficient similarities are apparent to draw a number of conclusions about the likely future efficiency of road freight in Egypt. The UK road freight industry was deregulated following the 1968 Transport Act and a significant privatisation took place when the National Freight Corporation was purchased by its employees in 1981. The wider macroeconomic or national features of these developments in road freight are reserved for the next chapter, and the focus of the current chapter will be solely on cost and efficiency aspects.

Following the advent of the Conservative government under Margaret Thatcher in 1979, there ceased to be any government involvement in the internal efficiency of private companies in the UK and, consequently, there is a shortage of government-sponsored or authoritative independent published research into the internal efficiency of the road freight industry. However, shortly before the accession of the Thatcher government, the Price Commission was undertaking efficiency investigations on behalf of the previous Labour government. In its report on the road haulage industry (Price Commission, 1977) it claimed that small road haulage operators had only rudimentary knowledge of costing often based on 'rule-of-thumb judgements', although larger operators were better. Button (1983) summed up the situation at that time by claiming that hauliers misperceive costs in four ways:

- Money or time cost may be too small to take into account.
- Variable costs are regarded as fixed costs.
- Hauliers are unaware of the connection between a particular action and its costs.
- Hauliers are unaware of changing cost conditions over time.

Hoppe (1980) even went as far as to state that 'high costs may result from bad route location decisions of 50 years ago'. This may have been an extreme conclusion but it encapsulates the low esteem in which parts of the road freight industry were held at that time. During the 1970s a higher proportion of road freight traffic in Great Britain[1] was carried by own account operators compared with nearly two decades later (see Table 5.1). Although a range of factors, including government regulation, may influence the decision of manufacturers, wholesalers or retailers to use third party

---

[1] This work generally refers to the United Kingdom (UK). However, some statistics more precisely refer to Great Britain (GB) which excludes Northern Ireland.

haulage operators, one important reason is the confidence they have in the operators to deliver on time. Where this confidence is lacking, as apparently in Egypt today, there is a tendency for shippers to make greater use of their own vehicles. Often own account operations are not costed effectively and the true costs of transport may be 'hidden' in other costs such as those of production. A survey undertaken in 1986 of nearly 500 operators found that hire and reward operators tend to calculate their costs in more detail than own account operators, although a surprisingly high proportion of both types of operator did not appear to know the costs of their basic operating unit, the vehicle (Hallett and Gray, 1987). The survey found that transport departments of own account operators may be cross-subsidised by other non-transport departments, exactly the same finding as a survey undertaken in Egypt in the early 1990s (Study of the National Transport System in Egypt, 1993). The British survey found that standing costs in particular may often be calculated annually, or at best quarterly or monthly, rather than weekly or daily. Published detailed studies of road freight costing do not exist for Egypt which does not have a tradition of business academic research. However, it would seem reasonable to assume that there is some correspondence with the UK findings, but with a 20 year time lag. The Egyptian Delphi panel agreed that under privatisation, identifying areas where cost reduction could be made is the main task for road freight management, and that improved profits will only be achieved after costs and service levels have been taken into account.

Table 5.1
Goods moved and lifted in Great Britain

	1958	1968	1973	1986	1996
Goods moved (% tonne-km)					
mainly hire and reward	52	60	64	68	74
mainly own account	48	40	36	32	26
Goods lifted (% tonnes)					
mainly hire and reward				55	62
mainly own account				45	38

Source: Adapted from DETR (1997), and Armitage (1980)

Age of vehicles

In 1992, the Egyptian state sector fleet amounted to 2,320 vehicles, with about 23.4 per cent of them less than four years old, and 31.8 per cent over eight years old (see Table 5.2). Table 5.3 shows the operational condition of the state sector fleet. Of the total fleet, only 67.5 per cent of vehicles were in use.

Table 5.2
State sector fleet by age in Egypt (1992)

	Direct Transport Company	Businesses Transport Company	Inland Transport Company	Heavy Transport Company	Goods Transport Company
< 2 Years	43	14	42	128	29
2-4 Years	93	44	16	87	48
4-6 Years	53	149	104	64	128
6-8 Years	141	67	102	80	148
8-10 Years	52	89	101	16	80
+10 Years	203	74	40	9	76
Total	**585**	**437**	**405**	**384**	**509**

Source: Holding Company for Transport (1993)

In developed economies, road freight vehicles would be assumed to have a useful life of about six or seven years by reputable companies, although trailers could be employed much longer. The problems of maintaining, repairing and insuring such fleets can be considerable, and it has become common practice for operators to lease such equipment from specialist leasing companies. This transfers the risk of ownership of the equipment to the leasing company. It also allows road freight operators to obtain more up-to-date vehicles and to adapt more easily to changing circumstances, thereby avoiding technological obsolescence (Minalan, 1998).

Table 5.3
State sector fleet by vehicle condition in Egypt (1992)

	Total	In operational condition	In use
Direct Transport Company	585	465	445
Transport Businesses Company	437	349	313
Inland Transport Company	405	366	357
Heavy Transport Company	384	315	290
Goods Transport Company	509	426	370
Total	**2320**	**1921**	**1775**

Source: Holding Company for Transport (1993)

Costing and competition

As mentioned earlier, all road freight operations in Egypt have been regulated since 1957. However, a stipulation regarding the regulation of pricing included in the law is not enforced. The Ministry of Transport may or may not enforce it as it sees fit, which means freedom for operators to price their service as they wish. As a result, the state sector road freight companies face considerable competition from the co-operatives, private sector companies, and other subsidised modes of freight transport, namely the railways and the inland water companies. This competition has resulted in a sharp fall in freight rates. The study carried out by the UN-ESCWA (1994), based on the financial statements of the state sector road haulage companies, shows that in 1993 the rates charged by them covered only 63 per cent of costs.

The unfair competition underlying this fall in freight rates could possibly be attributed to three specific reasons. First, subsidy of the railways and the inland water transport companies enabled them to offer lower prices. Second, the co-operatives used to get their contracts from the state sector road freight companies for a five per cent administration fee, increased to ten per cent by 1988. Since the establishment of the holding companies in 1991, the co-operatives have been able to tender directly, and save the ten per cent fee. As a result the co-operatives have become able to offer a much lower rate than the state sector companies. Third, many years ago before nationalisation of the road freight industry, legislation made a distinction between own account operators and professional operators, with the former unable to carry goods for others. The nationalisation law did not include this article. Therefore, following deregulation of foreign trade and cement distribution, and reform of the Agriculture Bank, own account operators in these sectors with relatively small fleets are now able to compete for tenders with professional hire and reward operators.

The Study of the National Transport System in Egypt (1993) indicates that transport costs in the own account sector are in general not treated independently, but as a part of production costs, thus enabling cross-subsidisation to take place. The UN-ESCWA study (1994) suggests that one of the problems associated with the state sector road freight industry in Egypt is an absence of the use of advanced costing systems and cost centre calculations, which would otherwise show the cost of the different types of vehicles, goods, and functions. The outcome of the current Egyptian system is that cross subsidisation enables own account operators to compete in tenders at low prices, sometimes unreasonably low, probably at the expense of quality of service, and thus against the long term future development of the industry.

According to data provided by the State Sector Information Centre (1995) all the state sector road freight companies continued to report losses for the three years 1992, 1993, and 1994 (with the exception of General Nile Company for Direct Transport in the year 1994). They have only been able to survive by incurring considerable debts, which amounted to LE 165 million in 1995 (Al-Ahram, 1996). The internal cost of the state sector road freight companies in Egypt was investigated by UN-ESCWA (1994). This study claimed that one of the most important problems facing road freight companies is an increase in costs without a parallel increase in freight rates. The study suggested two reasons for increased costs. First, there was an increase in the cost of fuel by 400 per cent and in wages by 40 per cent between 1988 and 1993. Second, the cost of purchasing both vehicles and spare parts has increased as a result of liberalisation of the currency exchange rate. It has also led to an increase in the cost of some other operating elements, which are mainly produced domestically, such as tyres and batteries, since most of their components are imported. The UN-ESCWA study only investigated state sector companies, but expected a better performance from the co-operatives and the existing private sector, due to the lower number of employees and lower depreciation cost, since the average age of vehicles is higher than in the state sector companies. The study also highlighted the inaccuracy of the annual reports of the state sector companies owing to the costing limitations mentioned above and an absence of information systems for use by different levels of management.

Logistics and supply chain management

Probably the most quoted definition of logistics is that of the Council of Logistics Management in the USA.

> Logistics is the process of planning, implementing and controlling the efficient, effective flow and storage of raw materials, in-process inventory, finished goods, services and related information from point of origin to point of consumption (including inbound, outbound, internal and external movements) for the purpose of conforming to customer requirements (Coyle *et al*, 1996, p.28).

The essence of this approach is that it *integrates* various transport modes, inventories, warehouse operations, materials handling systems and other activities in a systematic way, particularly enabling *cost trade-offs* to be made between the different elements. For example, high-value goods held in store incur high inventory costs based on the capital tied up in those goods. Therefore, it may be sensible to reduce inventory levels, but use a faster and more expensive form of transport to maintain efficient delivery or customer service. Transport costs rise, but overall logistics costs are reduced because of inventory cost savings. In other words there is a trade-off between transport and inventory.

Supply chain management is closely associated with the logistics approach. The supply chain, also called the logistics pipeline, may stretch beyond a single company and country and require close international co-ordination of all logistics activities to ensure a satisfactory level of service for the final customer in the supply chain. Christopher (1992) provides an example of a supply chain that could have direct relevance for Egypt as it concerns cotton products.

> The supply chain is the network of organisations that are involved, through upstream and downstream linkages, in the different processes and activities that produce value in the form of products and services in the hands of the ultimate consumer. Thus for example a shirt manufacturer is a part of a supply chain that extends upstream through the weavers of fabrics to the manufacturers of fibres, and downstream through distributors and retailers to the final consumer (Christopher, 1992, p.12).

Traditionally, such organisations did not co-operate closely but acted as independent trading companies with each other. Although this type of relationship is still widespread today, increasingly supply chains are becoming more integrated and members of the chain collaborate closely over inventory levels and locations, often through modern forms of communication such as electronic data interchange (EDI).

Transport, of course, forms an important part of the integrated supply system. The transport world has reacted to the logistics approach (and sometimes even encouraged it) by providing intermodal freight transport services. Intermodal transport has been defined as 'the seamless and continuous door-to-door transportation of freight on two or more transportation modes' (Muller, 1995, p.1). The objective of intermodal systems is to keep goods moving without any delays at ports or other terminals where goods are transferred from one transport mode to another. This has been made possible by the use of *unit load devices (ULDs)*, most notably the ISO container. Unit load devices enable cargo to be unitised into equipment (e.g. pallets, bags, boxes) ensuring faster handling. The International Standards Organisation (ISO) is responsible for determining world-wide standard sizes for containers and some other ULDs. In order to make ULDs operate effectively, it is essential that not only all associated equipment (vehicles, cranes, etc.) is appropriately standardised, but also that there is an effective process of transfer of shipping documentation and other information.

In developed countries the road freight industry has reacted to the logistics approach by offering a wider range of services than the traditional operator, who normally provided only transport. The provision of these services is sometimes called value-added logistics and includes warehousing, inventory maintenance, repackaging and labelling. The provision of such services is suitable mainly for large operators with an established reputation. Often operators provide a dedicated service, meaning that vehicles and other facilities are dedicated to a single customer or shipper, even to the extent of displaying that customer's logo on the vehicles during the extent of the contract. From the hauliers' point of view, contract distribution provides a guaranteed level of income, at least for the duration of the contract. From the manufacturers' point of view, capital previously locked in vehicle fleets, warehousing facilities, and staff to manage distribution activities will be released and reallocated to core activities.

If the privatisation of road haulage in Egypt is to be effective in its contribution to the economy it will need to provide modern services based on efficient logistics. The introduction of such logistics systems requires a heavy programme of investment by hauliers in vehicles, warehousing, electronic communications systems and other facilities. Egypt already has a large co-operative sector consisting mainly of owner-drivers. A further increase in the number of small operators with relatively little capital would not allow the development of these logistics systems. Therefore, the best approach to privatising the state sector road freight companies in Egypt from a logistics standpoint is probably as large scale entities, by transferring the companies' assets to shares sold through the stock exchange (or as workers' shares), or selling off the companies in their existing form through tenders.

The interface between land and sea transport

Effective logistics and supply chain management systems require efficient intermodal transport. Therefore, the privatised Egyptian road freight sector will need to interact with the ports and maritime sector.

State control over shipping was originally introduced under President Nasser in 1964. Law 12 enabled the state organisation, Martrans, to operate as a monopoly for all cargo bookings to and from Egypt and restricted the scope of the private sector (Lloyd's List, 1998). Although more private operations were permitted under President Sadat in 1973, a totally free market was not announced until 1997. The relative profitability of Egypt's maritime companies should ensure a rapid privatisation, probably before the end of 1998 with ten operating companies and two holding companies to be privatised, including three container handling companies and four ships' agencies (Lloyd's List, 1997a). In this sector 100 per cent foreign ownership is permitted, opening the door to large international companies able to offer global integrated shipping and logistics services.

As mentioned earlier, the efficient use of standardised ISO containers is central to effective intermodal transport. Egypt has three government-owned container handling companies based in Alexandria, Damietta and Port Said. They claim to run profitable businesses, although international port operators consider that capacity could be increased by up to 100 per cent with better management and relatively low additional capital. For example, the capacity of the port of Damietta could increase from 550,000 TEU per year to one million TEU with additional capital of only US $15 million (Lloyd's List, 1997a). A TEU is a 'twenty-foot equivalent unit', the standard measure for container capacity within a system. It refers to the length of a container so that, for example, a 40 foot long container is two TEU.

Existing private companies associated with maritime or intermodal transport appear to be thriving in the climate of liberalisation. For example, the shipping and freight forwarding company, Egytrans, was 60 per cent oversubscribed when it became the first maritime company to be listed on the Cairo stock exchange in October 1997 (Lloyd's List, 1997b). The company planned to build a container freight depot at Dikheila to handle 'less than container load' (LCL) cargo. This type of operation, also called consolidation or groupage, brings together smaller consignments from several, or even many shippers in a single container. It requires efficient transfer between sea and land services, including a rapid delivery system usually based on road haulage. Many problems need to be overcome before such an effective system exists in Egypt. Shipping agents were claiming in 1997 that the average time for clearing and inspection of cargo was 20 days, and the time for a container to turn round from arrival to departure sailing was 30 days (Lloyd's List, 1997b). These reported times are extremely slow and unacceptable for a modern intermodal transport system. Nevertheless, at the time of writing this book, the mood in the Egyptian maritime industry was optimistic. A combination of existing Egyptian maritime entrepreneurial skills with international management following privatisation may lead to better intermodal performance. A high quality road haulage sector will also be required.

This chapter has shown that one of the major changes that is required before a newly privatised road freight industry can be deemed efficient is a management which recognises the importance of costing. It has stressed that these costs must not only include all the elements of transport costs, but also the other costs involved in the wider logistics function. Logistics companies are required in developing countries if their distribution systems are to succeed, but such companies require huge amounts of investment, which is unlikely to be forthcoming if the industry is too fragmented.

6 Macroeconomic problems facing road freight privatisation

Introduction

If Egypt continues along the same path of widespread privatisation, many industries including road haulage will be in a state of flux for years to come. It is therefore difficult to predict what will be the eventual outcome, but valuable insights may be gained from comparing Egypt's road freight development with that of other countries, particularly where privatisation is further developed. Therefore, the approach adopted in this chapter is to compare the privatisation process of road freight in Egypt with that of the UK and Hungary. The UK has been selected because it was one of the first countries in the world to deregulate its road haulage industry under the Transport Act 1968, and it also has a well-documented history of road freight privatisation. Hungary has been chosen because it has many similarities with Egypt, and has progressed further down the road to privatisation.

Privatisation and road haulage in Britain

In 1979 the proportion of British industry owned and controlled by the state was at a high level. State-owned industries accounted for over one-seventh of total investment in the UK and were responsible for over ten per cent of the country's Gross Domestic Product (GDP). These industries dominated the transport, energy, communications, steel and shipbuilding sectors of the British economy. The state-owned industrial sector in Britain was largely created about 50 years ago under a Labour government with a socialist agenda following World War II. The motivation for its creation was partly political by bringing the 'commanding heights' of the economy into state ownership, and partly economic since the industries in question were inefficient and in need of rationalisation and reconstruction. However, the performance of British nationalised industries proved to be generally disappointing with a low return on capital employed, a poor record of productivity and manpower costs and a low level of customer satisfaction (Richardson, 1990).

In 1979, with a new, more capitalist-orientated Conservative government, Britain started its privatisation programme with a reduction of government shareholding in state-owned enterprises. The sale of shares took two forms; public offerings, such as British Aerospace, Cable and Wireless and Amersham International, and private sales such as British Rail Hotels (sold by British Railways) and International Aeradio (sold by British Airways). The aims of the privatisation programme in Britain changed as the programme developed. Indeed, the concept of privatisation was not contained in the Conservative Party manifesto for the 1979 election, nor was it an issue in the 1983 election (Wiltshire, 1987). Even by the middle of the 1980s there was no distinct policy document from the British government or the Conservative Party defining or justifying privatisation, or outlining the way forward. Nevertheless, in 1983 the government stated that privatisation was a key element of its economic strategy, and that it would lead to a fundamental shift in the balance between the state and private sectors, bringing about a profound change in attitudes within state industries, and opening up exciting possibilities for the consumer. There would be better pay and conditions for employees, and a new freedom for the management of the industries concerned. The privatisation programme was also intended to promote competition, to increase efficiency and to encourage wider share ownership. By 1985, the government was emphasising another major objective of privatisation, which was to bring a halt to the 'meddling' of ministers and politicians in general (Wiltshire, 1987).

By 1986, the government was talking in terms of 'further and faster', to increase business and economic efficiency by competition, rationalisation and restructuring and by carefully designed regulatory regimes. It is evident that the objectives of the privatisation programme changed over time and as the programme gathered momentum (Wiltshire, 1987).

Development of road freight privatisation in the UK

Although deregulation of an industry often precedes privatisation, the two processes may be combined and, therefore, they are considered together in this section. Deregulation of the freight sector is an issue of major importance in many countries of the world. Agreement was reached in 1988 amongst member states of the European Community (now the European Union) to deregulate the international freight sector. During the late 1980s a number of European countries (e.g. the Netherlands, Belgium and France) were in the process of deregulating their freight sectors in anticipation of the completion of the single European market in 1992 (Cooper, 1993). The UK formally deregulated road freight transport in the Transport Act of 1968, undoing the regulating legislation of the 1933 Road and Rail Traffic Act. Between 1933 and 1968, the 1947 Transport Act brought long distance hire and reward hauliers into state ownership, and the 1953 Transport Act instructed the British Transport Commission to sell off the nationally owned public fleet (Committee of Inquiry into Operators' Licensing, 1979). It can therefore be seen that there is not necessarily always an obvious relationship between deregulation and privatisation.

The origins of the carriers' licensing system in the UK lay in the rapidly changing transport market of the 1920s and early 1930s. At that time the railways, being the major carriers of goods, were subject to common carrier obligations and other strict controls which were designed to offset their monopoly, while road transport carried goods virtually free of constraint. By the late 1920s, there was a widespread feeling that some control of road haulage was necessary and that an inequitable and uneconomic distribution of goods between rail and road resulted from restrictions on the one and the freedom of the other.

During World War II the Road Haulage Organisation was established, consisting of most major long distance operators. The government controlled the road haulage industry through its control of this organisation, and this situation remained unchanged until the second half of the 1940s. The 1947 Transport Act brought long distance hire or reward operators into public ownership under the new British Transport Commission which was intended to provide a properly integrated system of public inland transport and port facilities within Britain (Wistrich, 1983). Road haulage was nationalised and long-distance lorries were operated as a public monopoly by British Road Services. Within this structure, public and contract carriers operated by private enterprise were licensed and restricted to operations within 25 miles of their bases, but firms which ran lorries solely to transport their own goods were left entirely free of such restrictions. The aim of road haulage regulation was to prevent open competition between road and rail over the long-distance hauls and to regulate it over the shorter distances. The 1953 Transport Act empowered the British Transport Commission to sell off its fleet of 41,000 vehicles. In the event, they were unable to find buyers for all the vehicles and were allowed to retain and operate a fleet of 7,000 vehicles. Under the 1962 Transport Act, British Road Services and the rest of the nationalised fleet were transferred to the Transport Holding Company (Maltby and White, 1982).

The National Freight Corporation: a case study of privatisation The 1968 Transport Act, introduced under a Labour government, removed quantity constraints on entry into the road haulage industry which had existed since 1933, and replaced them with quality constraints. The 1968 Act also aimed to integrate freight services throughout the country, and to achieve that the National Freight Corporation was set up to take over all state-owned road freight units. Various nationalised road freight companies, including the British Rail road fleet, were integrated into the corporation, which took over a workforce of about 66,000 people and a fleet of about 30,000 vehicles. Some of these integrated companies were loss-making, such as the renamed National Carriers with losses of about £20 million on a turnover of £25 million in 1968. Since the government recognised that the new National Freight Corporation inherited considerable losses as a result of the transfer of the British Rail road freight activities to it, the National Freight Corporation received five years' subsidy to help with the losses of the former rail-road freight company.

The Corporation started a reorganisation, reducing the workforce and the number of vehicles substantially between 1968 and 1979. By 1972 reform was undertaken towards decentralisation and seven regional companies were set up. However, as a result of the 1968 Transport Act, which liberalised entry to the road freight industry, the price-cutting competition from new private sector companies was tough and resulted in reduced profits. The National Freight Corporation had a difficult time and the improvements achieved were not maintained during the recession of 1974/75. In 1975 losses from two subsidiaries of the Corporation, namely British Road Services and Pickfords, drove the Corporation into operating losses of over £31 million (Thompson, 1990). Owing to the financial difficulties of the National Freight Corporation, the government appointed a financial consultant in 1975 to examine the Corporation's finances, resulting in a top management reorganisation (McLachlan, 1983). In 1978 government help, in addition to some other forms of relief, enabled £53 million of the Corporation's capital debt to be written off, leaving debt of £100 million. This assistance enabled the Corporation to achieve profits of £20.8 million in 1978.

In the summer of 1979, the Conservative Party published its election manifesto, specifically naming the National Freight Corporation, among others, as a candidate for sale of shares to the public. The National Freight Corporation Board advocated privatisation by selling its shares in the stock market as a single entity, including National Carriers. This was both to take advantage of the value of National Carriers' mainly city-centre properties, and to avoid creating a subsidised competitor. The National Freight Corporation also wanted the government to fund its pension schemes, and write off the debt from the balance sheet.

As a result of recession, the volume of goods carried by the Corporation fell, as did profits. The Corporation had no hope of a successful flotation in the stock market at that time, thus making a management buy-out a more attractive proposition. This resulted in a proposal by Barclays Bank to lend the Corporation employees £55 million to buy the company, and provide a further £70 million for working capital. An employee buy-out is a transaction by which a company is sold to people involved in running the company. Three economic outcomes are likely to follow. The employee equity participation should increase wage flexibility, employee ownership should have positive effects on employment levels, and it should also harmonise workplace relations, resulting in improving labour productivity and performance (Nejad, 1986).

Under the 1980 Transport Act, the National Freight Company Limited replaced the Corporation. The government wrote off the remaining £100 million of capital debt of the company. In order to allow company employees to use company assets as a security, the 1981 Companies Act was passed. The government agreed to sell the company to its employees for £53.5 million, conditional upon raising at least about £4.2 million, of which about £2.2 million had to be in cash, and the remainder through the employees' loan scheme (Thompson, 1990).

The employee buy-out of the National Freight Corporation is unique in the history of road freight privatisation in Britain. The employees and pensioners of the corporation were able to raise the necessary funds to buy the company from the government, instead of putting its shares in the stock market. In 1985 a research project took place to study this buy-out and came to two main conclusions. The employees in an employee-owned firm are likely to be more co-operative than in a conventional business, and given the opportunity to participate in a management led employee buy-out, the response of the employees is likely to be related to their access to relevant information (Nejad, 1986). By 1986, the company introduced a new profit-sharing scheme to improve performance with some 80 per cent of the workforce participating (Key Note, 1992). The company went on to be one of the most successful international groups specialising in the provision of logistics and transport systems, operating in about 20 countries around the world under the three main divisions of transport, logistics and home delivery services. Employees who participated in the buy-out made huge profits of around 100 times their original investment. NFC (as it is now called) has experienced some problems in the 1990s, including a substantial change of its management and new external appointments. In 1995 it restructured its transport and logistics operations to achieve greater management accountability in each unit. Despite problems it continued to be Britain's largest distribution company in 1994/95 with a turnover of £2,200 million (Key Note, 1996).

Privatisation and road haulage in Hungary

Hungary is a landlocked state located in East-Central Europe at the cross roads of major trade routes both from north to south between the Baltic and the Mediterranean Seas, and east to west between Russia and the European Union. In such a location it has always played a major role in transit traffic by road and rail (Roe, 1992). Hungary is used as a comparison with Egypt because it is a country which is going through the processes of privatisation and deregulation, and in addition has a promising road freight industry. As such, it appears to have many similarities with Egypt, but also some significant differences.

After World War II, the command economy of the USSR was imposed in various forms in other Eastern European countries resulting in rapid industrialisation. In socialist Eastern Europe there was some apparent success in catching up with the West, and East European economies played a growing international role in heavy manufacturing industry in the 1950s and 1960s. However, the growth of electronics, software development and services as major business sectors revealed the weaknesses of centrally planned economies, unable to achieve the rate of technological progress and innovation of the market economies of the West and Japan (Welfens, 1992). In 1991, the Eastern Bloc's Council of Mutual Economic Assistance (CMEA) was dissolved, and the USSR's history ended with the re-emergence of Russia and other former Soviet states, and the creation of the Commonwealth of Independent States. After more than four decades of socialism, Eastern European countries started a process intended to transform themselves into market economies (Welfens, 1992).

In Hungary economic reforms, particularly in agriculture, had started much earlier. Compulsory plan targets and deliveries for agriculture were abolished as early as the late 1950s and a number of products were sold in open farm markets. In manufacturing industry, following the 1956 Hungarian uprising, radical steps were taken to improve the economy with the aim of increasing production by introducing new machinery and decreasing costs. The command structure was decentralised and plant managers became more independent and were encouraged to operate profitably, applying realistic and achievable plans (Narkiewicz, 1986). Five-year plans provided the broad framework of economic development, while operational managers of enterprises were given annual or quarterly plans based on sales or output targets, allocations of the major material inputs and cost reduction targets (Hare *et al*, 1981).

The mid-1960s saw a further turning point for the Hungarian economy with the re-emergence of economic tensions, such as increasing disequilibrium in the balance of trade and payments. The major reform was associated with the New Economic Mechanism of 1968 (Berend and Ranki, 1985). This aimed to replace plan directives with a form of market relations among firms, by reducing central price determination, linking domestic prices of exports and imports to prices in the world market, and decentralising a major part of investment decisions (World Bank, 1982). Although the central plan continued to determine overall economic policy, enterprises were given greater independence to make employment, production and investment decisions. The government used indirect controls such as prices, the exchange rate, credit availability and monetary and fiscal policy to harmonise the objectives of the central plan and individual enterprises (Lloyds Bank, 1986).

During the 1970s there was a significant change when the world recession, inflation and the rise in price of oil and other raw materials brought a sharp deterioration to Hungary's economy. An increase in central government direction and intervention followed to insulate Hungary from world events, so some degree of recentralisation took place during the 1970s. A further change in direction came after a record balance of payments deficit in 1978, when the authorities reacted by resuming the process of decentralising decision-making as a means to correct distortions in the pricing system (Lloyds Bank, 1986).

In 1988 Hungary introduced the foundations of a Western style tax system, including value added tax (Frydman *et al*, 1993). The Company Act of 1989 allowed state-owned companies to form joint stock companies, private persons to form limited liability companies, and foreigners to buy shares in Hungarian companies. After the May 1990 general election, the Hungarian government started its privatisation programme with the aim of reducing the share of state-owned assets in the competitive sector to about 50 per cent.

The first step towards privatisation was the so-called 'Pre-Privatisation Programme', known as 'spontaneous' or 'self-privatisation', resulting from management action, where the responsibility of privatising the enterprises is given to the companies' directors (Lieberman, 1994). This programme was intended to privatise retail trade, catering and service activities, and could be carried out quickly and successfully, since many enterprises had already been leased or hired by their managers under the liberalisation measures introduced during the 1980s (Lindsay, 1992). In fact, this form of privatisation proved unpopular because of allegations of profiteering with state properties simply being handed over to former Communist officials (Lieberman, 1994). As a result, by the end of 1990 the government created the State Property Agency (SPA), supervised by a government minister. Its duties include overseeing the sale of state property and approving any sales of assets. Under this system of privatisation, state-owned enterprises were transformed into limited liability companies and then offered for sale by tender. By December 1992 the State Property Agency had approved the privatisation of 679 companies, representing a property value of approximately US $14.5 billion. Independent of the State Property Agency, 299 enterprises succeeded in self-privatisation, and 298 companies privatised through the establishment of joint ventures (Murray, 1994).

Also by the end of 1992, a second organisation was set up to assist the State Property Agency. The Hungarian State Holding Company was set up to take over 184 of Hungary's strategic industries, such as power generation, railways, steel, and telecommunications (Euromoney, 1995). The key difference between the two institutions is that the State Holding Company was charged with management of those companies in which the state would retain a stake, while the State Property Agency was responsible for the companies which were to be fully privatised (Euromoney, 1994). In 1994, the Europe Review reported that the State Property Agency was losing its momentum after an initial burst of activity, during which many of the best-known companies in the country were sold off. The State Property Agency became a main target for the press, because of its large staff turnover and poor performance (Europe Review, 1994). It was also blamed for the poor performance of the Budapest Stock Market, where there were only 25 traded stocks after three years of operation. In May 1995, the Hungarian Parliament approved a new privatisation law where responsibility for selling state assets was placed under the control of a Privatisation Minister (Budapest Sun, 1995).

Road freight transport has been a component in the Hungarian privatisation process. The role of the Ministry of Transport has moved from detailed planning and management to overseeing the actions of the various companies that are being set up in the transport field. With the processes of liberalisation and economic reform, the number of small goods and public transport companies has been increased. The growth in the number of goods vehicle operators occurred after the dissolution in 1983 of the state-owned trust of which Volan, the largest road freight operator, was part. Before that, Volan worked mainly domestically, and owned 30 per cent of the lorries and had over 50 per cent of the weight capacity. After 1983, Volan had only nine per cent of lorries and 30 per cent of the capacity (Mackett, 1992).

Egypt compared with the UK and Hungary

This section compares the privatisation programmes and the road freight industry under the three different systems of the UK, Hungary and Egypt. The objective is to determine whether lessons can be learnt from the British and Hungarian experiences that are valid for Egypt. Although all three countries differ considerably in many ways, there are certain features of privatisation, particularly of road freight, that appear common to different societies.

Privatisation

The objective behind privatisation, in both market and non-market economies, is to reduce state involvement in industry and commerce, with the aim of increasing the efficiency of the economy. Private ownership is assumed to provide the incentive to improve cost efficiency, and private companies should emphasise cost reduction and a high level of productivity (Ghosh, 1994; Bos, 1993; Liu, 1995). In the UK, Egypt and Hungary, increased efficiency has been a clearly stated objective of the privatisation programmes, although other objectives include fund raising for the treasury, encouraging employees to own shares in their companies, and strengthening the capital market. In market economies, privatisation takes place within the same socio-economic framework so that it simply requires the transfer of ownership from state to private sector. This means that, given the appropriate political climate, privatisation in such countries can be a speedy process. In non-market economies, where privatisation is a part of the wider operation of economic reform, a distinction is usually made between the two strategies or scenarios of shock therapy or gradual transition. The gradual transition approach has been adopted by both Egypt and Hungary, where the process of setting up the framework of a market economy took place during the 1980s prior to the privatisation process.

Sachs and Woo (1994) claim that Poland applied the shock therapy approach and suffered for it initially, but growth returned to its economy, whereas Hungary, with its gradual transition approach saw economic decline by the mid 1990s. These results are supported by statistics from the Hungarian National Bank, quoted in Chikan (1996), see Table 6.1.

Table 6.1

Table 6.1
Change in GDP (percentage of 1989 figures)

Country	1990	1991	1992	1993	1994
Hungary	96.5	85.0	81.4	79.5	82.3
Poland	88.4	81.7	82.9	86.1	90.4

Source: The World Economy and International Finances, 12 April 1995,
Hungarian National Bank, Budapest, (adapted from Chikan, 1996)

However, output and unemployment should not be the only criteria on which success is judged; other social costs should also be taken into account. For example, real wages and real savings declined less in Hungary than in Poland, and the strategy contributed to political stability, whereas in Poland the deep recession destabilised the political system to some extent. Thus, the gradual approach to privatisation seems to have helped Hungary to avoid great social tensions (Adam, 1995). This has been the reason for application of this approach in Egypt, where the government has tried to minimise the social cost of transition.

Comparison of national road freight industries

The road freight industry in all three countries is highly fragmented, dominated by large numbers of small firms, with a small number of large firms. In contrast to Britain, where there is now no state sector in the road freight industry, in both Egypt and Hungary the road freight industry consists of state and private sector companies, and co-operatives. However, there is a difference in practice between the co-operatives in Egypt and in Hungary, since the co-operatives in Egypt, unlike in Hungary, do not own the capital of the co-operative. Instead the capital is owned privately by the members, so that the co-operative sector in Egypt could be seen as a collection of private small firms.

The co-operative sector dominates the road freight hire and reward market in Egypt, with 70.2 per cent of total goods lifted by road in 1992. This domination is a result of the liberalisation of foreign trade, resulting in an increase in the demand for small rather than large operators. In contrast, in Hungary the state sector dominates the road freight market, with 68.6 per cent of total goods lifted in 1993.

Hire and reward (or professional) road freight companies dominate the market in Britain, accounting for 57.6 per cent of total goods lifted and

72.5 per cent of total goods moved in 1993. In contrast, own account transport dominates the road freight market in Hungary. The hire and reward haulage sector in Hungary lost about one-quarter of its market during the early 1990s mainly because of low quality of service. According to Hungarian Ministry of Transport data, shares of hire and reward haulage declined between 1990 and 1993 by 25.9 per cent in terms of tonnage, and by 23.4 per cent in terms of freight volume. Unfortunately, equivalent data is not available for Egypt. However, it has been estimated that in Egypt in 1990 about 60 per cent of total haulage capacity was carried by own account operators, with about 35 per cent by the state sector and by government ministries, and about 25 per cent by the private sector (Study of the National Transport System in Egypt, 1993).

The move towards hire and reward haulage in Britain, and towards own account operators in both Hungary and Egypt could be explained by the quality of service offered by the industry. In Britain the growing share of hire and reward haulage, at the expense of the own account operators, occurred mainly during the 1980s as a result of the growing number of manufacturers and retailers choosing to contract out their transport requirements to operators in the hire and reward sector, not only for transport but also for warehousing facilities. In Hungary, with the tide of privatisation and foreign investment, the quality of service provided by hire and reward operators could not meet customer requirements satisfactorily, particularly with more western investment in the country, requiring a high standard of service including delivery. Nevertheless, delivery efficiency in Hungary has improved considerably since 1986, with the average number of days late for delivery diminishing from 33 days in 1986, through 21.4 days in 1991, to 9 days in 1994 (Chikan, 1996).

The nature of inventories in Hungary has also changed, with a move away from materials or parts for production to finished goods inventories. Inventories of materials and purchased parts as a percentage of all inventories fell from 68.3 per cent in 1986 to 57 per cent in 1994. Over the same period, finished goods inventories rose from 13.8 per cent to 24 per cent. The remaining inventory is work-in-progress, which remained fairly static over the same period (Chikan, 1996). Such developments are typical of transitional economies in Eastern Europe, and there is little reason to doubt that they apply to many privatising economies. Market economies place greater emphasis on customer satisfaction, which requires availability of finished goods. The danger is that finished goods stocks may become too high through failure or poor performance in the supply chain. Lower stock levels, while maintaining delivery speed and reliability, can be achieved through the use of efficient logistics providers. Hungary is taking steps in this direction with, among other developments, the establishment of the Hungarian

Association of Logistics, Purchasing and Inventory Management in 1991 as a response to the transitional process, and offering logistics courses to management (Chikan, 1996). Although Egypt does not have a national logistics association, the Egyptian National Institute of Transport (ENIT) has started to offer logistics courses developed in part by the authors of this book.

In Egypt, the high share of own account operators of road freight could also be explained by the poor quality of service offered by hire and reward hauliers. The survey undertaken by the Study of the National Transport System in Egypt (1993), showed that the priority for companies was the safe and speedy transport of their raw materials and products. Thus, they rely on their own fleets due to the fear that the hire and reward companies could not be completely depended on.

The Delphi panel in Egypt was asked about the potential for professional hauliers in Egypt. The panel's agreement that a privatised, deregulated road freight industry requires a legal distinction to be made by the government between own account and professional operators is significant. At present, own account operators are undercutting the prices of professional state-owned operators, because they are able to cross-subsidise their costs from one department to another, and own account transport may be perceived as part of the total production costs. Privatised and deregulated road freight systems in developed countries such as the UK have shown a decline in own account transport for many years as professional hauliers have become more efficient. Even though own account operators are permitted to carry the goods of others, this seldom happens. The Egyptian experts in the Delphi panel appear to require the professional haulage sector to be protected from loss of business and this again reflects a lack of faith in the professional sector.

In order to improve the quality of the road freight industry, the Hungarian government passed a new law in May 1995. One of the major features of this law is that all owners, drivers and management of road freight companies have to take businesses courses, and also demonstrate competence. Previously, goods vehicle drivers needed only a drivers' licence, and there were no specific qualifications required for the owners and management. According to the new regulation, both owners and management must be qualified to run road freight businesses. The law also favours large and modern road freight companies, by demanding a minimum capital sum needed to establish a road freight company. According to the secretary-general of the National Association of Transport, the minimum capital regulation will force a lot of small companies out of the market (Budapest Sun, 1995). This competence requirement compares with the UK's Certificate of Professional Competence and the requirements for an Operators' Licence (Lowe, 1991). In Egypt there are no particular qualifications required to establish and/or run a road freight company, as well as no minimum capital regulation. Such regulation may be needed to produce a better quality of road freight service, as well for the development of the industry. With the privatisation of the road freight industry, the government in Egypt may need to consider and implement such regulations.

This chapter has looked at the history of road freight privatisation and discussed the relationship between deregulation and privatisation in the UK. Privatisation in the UK was eventually carried out through a management/employee buy-out of the major state-run company, but this was not an easy process and took several years to accomplish, and involved the writing off of substantial debts before privatisation could take place. It has, however, been judged by most commentators to be a success both for those who purchased shares, and for the company as a whole. The road freight sector in the UK is probably one of the most efficient in the world. One reason for this is that there are several large companies with the funds to make the required major investment in the wider logistics functions. If privatisation in Egypt is to be successful, it is possible that the state sector companies should be purchased as larger units able to provide the competition required for effective development to take place. Only in this way will the manufacturing sector increase its confidence in the 'professional' road freight sector.

7   External costs of road haulage

Introduction

Externalities are those costs or benefits that arise when the activities of one group affect the welfare of another group without any payment being made by the group creating the cost (Talley, 1988).   A distinction is made between technological and pecuniary externalities.   The latter result from a change in the prices of inputs or outputs in the economy, and which affect others financially, but do not produce misallocation of resources, given perfect competition.   The technological externalities include costs and benefits for which there is no market, for example the negative externalities of transport such as pollution (Baumol and Oates, 1988; Worcester, 1972).   Since pecuniary externalities do not affect resource allocation, the main concern of this chapter will be directed towards technological externalities.

Kapp (1972) defined externalities as losses caused by productive activities and borne by third persons, or cost elements shifted to society as a whole.   For Rothengatter (1994), externalities occur if the production or consumption function 'contains independent variables which are not controlled by the decision maker' (p.327).   The existence of externalities leads to a deviation from the neo-classical economic theory, in which the optimal resource allocation is achieved by the price mechanism (Verhoef, 1994).   In order to achieve optimal resource allocation all costs including externalities must be internalised.   Pigou's formula to internalise externalities in order to correct market failure relies on imposing a tax on the production of external diseconomies, and subsidising the production of external economies (Dietz and Stratten, 1992).   However, it is accepted that externalities may exist in the absence of property rights (Baumol and Oates, 1988).   Coase claims that where every asset is owned, the externalities would be internalised, but where there are some common goods, the payments would be arranged through the valuation and enforcement of the relevant property rights (Coase, 1960).   The basic difference between the Pigou and Coase approaches lies in the mechanism of internalising the externalities. The Pigou approach relies on taxes, while the Coase approach relies on the market itself or the legal system (Demsetz, 1964; Helm and Pearce, 1990).

Road transport externalities may be considered under the two main components of external costs and external benefits. The external costs include, first, the impact of the transport sector on the stock of non-renewable resources, which occurs because environmental resources are used to produce transport services without compensation, and, second, the interactions within the transport sector, resulting from the use of transport networks. The most popular example of the latter is road congestion, where each user entering the system affects the other users and contributes to a suboptimal user pattern of the network (Verhoef, 1994; Rothengatter, 1994). Rothengatter (1994) presents a number of external benefits of road transport. Those specifically related to freight transport include:

- Extension of the consumption pattern and improvement of living standards.

- Introduction of growth and structural effects, and freight logistics to create new approaches to industrial labour division and interaction, setting new quality standards such as 'just-in-time' transport.

- Increase in flexibility and innovation which creates a new quality of service and transport and strengthens the economy for international competition.

- Cost reductions for packing, processing, and logistics.

- Positive employment effects in peripheral regions.

These external benefits of road transport would, to some extent, compensate for the external costs and should also be taken into account. However, Kageson (1993) points out that serious analysis of the 'external' benefits of road transport shows that they are almost entirely internal benefits to the users or normal market effects of the type which occur in all markets. External benefits 'which are not reflected in market processes and therefore theoretically call for government intervention are quantitatively of absolutely no importance' (Kageson, 1993, p.39). For Verhoef (1994), the claimed external benefits of road transport are 'actually pecuniary benefits' resulting from lower transport costs or greater efficiency of road transport in comparison with other modes of transport. Verhoef (1994) concluded that there are no significant external benefits of road transport activities, and those external benefits, mentioned earlier, do not compensate for the external costs of road transport.

There is an extensive literature on the external costs of transport such as noise and air pollution and a review of such costs will be made later in this chapter. Most studies associated with external costs have normally been undertaken in developed countries. As such, they are sometimes claimed to be a particular concern of rich countries that have more or less resolved their problems of extreme economic poverty and now wish to improve 'secondary' areas of concern such as the environment. At the same time, rich countries may not wish to reduce their level of industry-generated pollution so that their standard of living suffers significantly. In particular, they may be reluctant to reduce the level of energy use by both cars and road freight. The difference in energy use for a selection of countries is shown in Table 7.1.

Table 7.1
Energy used by the transport sector (1993)

Country	Energy consumption per '000 population (TJ)	Energy consumption of transport sector as a % of total
Albania	3	17
Poland	9	14
Hungary	10	15
France	33	29
UK	34	31
USA	82	38

Source: United Nations Economic Commission for Europe (1996)

Thus, the average person in the USA uses 27 times as much energy on transport as the average person in Albania, and energy consumption on transport as a percentage of the total energy used in the USA is twice that of Albania.

Elements of external costs

The external costs of transport as a whole and road freight transport in particular are many and varied. Himanen *et al* (1992) state that external costs include noise, air pollution and lack of safety. For Banister and Button (1993), and Button (1993), the environmental implications of transport are noise, vibration, accident risk, atmospheric pollution, excess depletion of natural resources, community severance, water pollution, congestion and visual intrusion and aesthetics. Sharp and Jennings (1976) give the main components of the environmental costs which are caused by lorries as noise, air pollution, road wear, accident involvement, effects on roadside buildings (either by direct contact or through vibration), visual intrusion and delays caused to other road users. Button and Pearman (1981) claim two broad types of road freight external cost; congestion costs and pollution costs. Pollution costs include noise, air pollution, accidents, vibration, visual intrusion and community severance.

Potter (1997) considers external costs in terms of their area of impact and comes up with the classification shown in Table 7.2.

Table 7.2
Areas of impact of external costs

Area of Impact	Transport Sources
Local, e.g. noise, smell, air quality, health effects	Particulates, volatile organic compounds (VOCs), carbon monoxide, ozone, noise
Regional, e.g. waste disposal, land use	Landtake infrastructure
Continental, e.g. acid rain	Nitrogen oxides, sulphur dioxide
Global, e.g. climate change, ozone depletion	Carbon dioxide, ozone, CFCs

Source: Potter (1997)

In developing countries, the major problems probably arise from the local and global elements of the classification in Table 7.2. It is upon these that we will concentrate in the remainder of the chapter. The local element will be divided into the following:

- The environment (noise and pollution)
- The infrastructure (vibration and road wear)
- Social considerations (safety, congestion, intrusion and community severance).

Global warming

Global warming is currently a major topic of debate world-wide. Attention was focused on the issue following the 1992 United Nation's Rio Declaration on Environment and Development and the 1997 Kyoto summit.

Global warming is caused by carbon dioxide and other 'greenhouse' gases (such as methane, nitrous oxides and clorofluorocarbons). The greenhouse effect is so termed because a greenhouse allows in heat from the sun, but the glass reduces the ability of the heat to escape. Some gases emitted into the atmosphere have this same effect in reducing the ability of the heat to escape (Goodwin *et al*, 1991). Houghton (1994) and others summarise the possible impacts of global warming as:

- a rise of the sea level
- changes of climatic zones, for example desert regions
- greater unpredictability of weather systems
- global dying of wood
- detrimental effects on water resources
- increasing problems for agricultural production.

Many of these will have a direct impact on developing countries. There is a tendency for representatives of rich developed countries, with an already high standard of living, to require poor developing countries to cut back on greenhouse gases before obtaining a satisfactory standard of living. According to a report in the Economist of 21 March 1998, well-meaning environmentalists in the richer countries may often oppose developments in poorer countries such as the construction of large dams, an opposition which is to the disadvantage of the people of the developing country. They are concerned about the impact on other countries of environmental damage caused by 'global warming' or 'the greenhouse effect'. Under international agreement, such as at the Kyoto conference of 1997, richer countries have agreed to set targets limiting emissions of gases released by the use of fossil fuels, and developing countries are being pressed to set targets as well. Developing countries make the counter-argument that the richer countries, as the prime consumers of fossil fuels, should pay for any move to reduce their use. Rich countries are the main global polluters. Of course, in most developing countries the main immediate problem is to overcome the human suffering caused by poverty, and environmental measures that restrict the use of fossil fuels may also restrict economic growth.

Local external costs

The environment - pollution Many developing countries have an immediate environmental problem through polluted water and air. The Economist (21 March 1998) claims that the cost of pollution in some developing countries is already very high, quoting as an example a World Bank study in 1997 that estimated the cost of air and water pollution in China at $54 billion a year or eight per cent of the country's GDP.

Air pollution exists in Egypt, notably in the capital city of Cairo, which is one of the most polluted cities in the world. Among developing countries Egypt is one of the most urbanised. All countries in the world are classified by the World Bank according to per capita gross national product (GNP) as low income, middle income or high income. In 1992, Egypt was placed near the top of the low-income economies with a GNP of $640 per capita, just below Indonesia. Only about 35 countries have a lower per capita GNP than Egypt (World Bank, 1994). Of all the low-income economies, Egypt has the highest percentage (23 per cent in 1992) of its population living in urban agglomerations of one million or more. Therefore, in terms of air pollution Egypt has the double disadvantage of poverty and high urbanisation. A large part of Egypt's urban air pollution is caused by traffic including road freight. The privatisation process is likely to aggravate this problem unless there are environmental controls or transport users assume some responsibility for the external costs incurred by them. Unfortunately, there appears to be as yet little government action on the problem of air pollution and, indeed, the Environment Law of 1994 did not have a section on road transport, concentrating instead on maritime and River Nile pollution, and on industrial firms. To some extent this attitude is understandable in a developing country. Transport, both the ownership of private cars and road freighting of goods, is a highly visible indication of rising prosperity. Environmental measures that limit this development may not be welcome.

It is difficult to assess the contribution of road traffic to pollution levels. However, it has been estimated that in the UK, transport accounts for 77 per cent of carbon monoxide emissions, 57 per cent of nitrogen oxides, 51 per cent of black smoke, 38 per cent of VOC's, 28 per cent of particulate PM10s, 26 per cent of carbon dioxide and 4 per cent of sulphur dioxide (DETR, 1997a). It is even more difficult to assess the contribution of freight transport to total transport emissions. Table 7.3 compares emissions for cars and goods vehicles, again for the UK.

It can be seen from Table 7.3 that, in comparison to the average car, goods vehicles emit many more oxides of nitrogen, particulates and carbon dioxide per vehicle km, but fewer hydrocarbons and carbon monoxide. It must also be noted that because goods vehicles use diesel, they emit no lead. However, recent evidence suggests that the particulates emitted by diesel vehicles are particularly harmful to health.

The level of pollution emissions from vehicles depends very much on their state of repair. As Haq (1997) suggests, motor vehicles in developing countries tend to be in poor condition and badly maintained, with poor quality fuels. In addition, roads are poorer and traffic management is less well refined. It can therefore be surmised, that emissions from goods vehicles in developing countries are far higher than suggested below.

Table 7.3
Index of emissions for road vehicles (per vehicle kilometre)
in urban conditions

	Carbon monoxide	Hydro-carbons	Oxides of nitrogen	Particulates	Carbon dioxide
Petrol car : (without catalytic converter)	100	100	100	100	100
Goods Vehicles:					
3.5 - 7 tonnes	10	23	302	655	256
7.5 - 17 tonnes	17	17	424	528	325
> 17 tonnes	20	19	650	524	514

Source: From DETR (1997a)

Although there have been no specific studies of road freight transport as a cause of pollution in Cairo, one of the authors has published research on traffic pollution associated with car ownership in Cairo (Cullinane and Cullinane, 1995), and it is fair to say that the findings on pollution of this research apply as much to road freight as to other forms of road transport. There is a shortage of official statistics on pollution levels in Cairo but it is clear that the problem is serious. A report was prepared on behalf of the German Embassy (Stumpenhorst, 1992) outlining the results of various Egyptian health and environmental research in Cairo and the following statistics derive from that report. In 1983, Professor Nasralla of the National Research Institute in Cairo found that people in general living in Cairo had a blood lead absorption level of 30.5 microgrammes per decilitre (µg/dl), compared with normal levels of 10 to 15 µg/dl. Certain exposed groups such as traffic police had much higher levels. Cairo has a particular problem with accumulations of lead since it has a very low rainfall to wash lead out of the road dust. Rural areas of Egypt do not suffer from this form of pollution.

Carbon monoxide is also a dangerous product of traffic pollution, reducing the amount of oxygen in body tissues and consequently lowering both human motor skills and intellectual abilities. In the USA the Environmental Protection Agency provides an Air Pollution Standard Index, quoting a National Ambient Air Quality Standard (NAAQS) of ten milligrams of carbon monoxide per cubic metre (mg/m^3). Higher levels will damage the health of some people. A study in 1978 in Cairo found maximum levels of 42 mg/m^3 in a residential area and 104 mg/m^3 on a main road. According to the

NAAQS the former level is within the *warning* band and the latter is within the most dangerous band where *significant harm* will result from exposure and 'all persons should remain indoors, keeping windows and doors closed. All persons should minimise physical exertion and avoid traffic'.

More recently, positive steps have been taken to control air pollution in Cairo. Unleaded petrol has been sold at the same price as leaded petrol since 1997, and there has been a move towards the use of natural gas as a fuel, particularly for public transport. Encouraged by the government, a joint venture enterprise has been established to convert engines to run on both petrol and natural gas, served by a network of natural gas filling stations. This is partly because large reservoirs of natural gas have been found in the North Delta region, but it is also aimed at reducing air pollution, and saving oil for export.

Noise Noise can be defined as unwanted sound. It is this that causes a problem in terms of measurement, since what is unwanted by one group of people may not be unwanted by another. As the Committee on the Problem of Noise (1963) chaired by Sir Alan Wilson stated, noise 'is a matter rather of human values and environments than of precise physical measurement'. Cone and Hayes (1984) define noise as a 'sound that produces undesirable physical or psychological effects'. Traffic noise is measured on the 'A-Weighted decibel scale (dBA)', where the different frequencies of sound energy are weighted in proportion to the sensitivity of the human ear (Ogden, 1992). Larger engines and tyres mean more noise and, as Armitage (1980) states 'lorries, and especially the heaviest lorries, make a large contribution to the peaks of traffic noise which cause particular annoyance' (p.30). Sharp and Jennings (1976) consider noise caused by road freight operations as one of the most serious of the social costs imposed by lorries. Himanen *et al* (1992) point out that studies in various countries show a relatively high level of social costs of traffic noise ranging from 0.06 per cent to 0.12 per cent of the GDP. Button (1993) says that studies in the Netherlands suggested that the number of people claiming moderate disturbance from road traffic noise rose from 48 per cent to 60 per cent between 1977 and 1987.

While international comparisons show evidence of decline in numbers suffering from serious noise problems (that is over 65 dBA) in some countries, it also provides evidence that the numbers in other countries have risen (Button, 1993). Noise has an influence through its dimensions of frequency, amplitude, complexity and duration and spacing (Cone and Hayes, 1984). Banister and Button (1993) state that noise has several different effects on health and well being and affects activities such as communications and sleep. These effects further induce psychological and physiological disorders such as stress, tiredness and sleep disturbance. Ogden (1992) defines six factors contributing to the traffic noise levels. They are vehicle speed, traffic flow, traffic operation, road surface, weather, and vehicle type and conditions.

The infrastructure These comprise two main elements, vibration and road wear. Although vibration may cause damage to buildings, there are a number of factors such as weather conditions and shrinkage of materials which also contribute to it. Therefore, it is not easy to isolate the effect of traffic vibration on buildings from the other effects. Road wear is caused by heavy traffic, but again, the effect of goods vehicles is not easy to isolate from the effect of other transport modes.

Vibration Armitage (1980) states that there are two types of traffic induced vibration; ground-borne, originating in the road surface, and air-borne caused by low frequency sound emitted from vehicles. Most of the problems arise from ground-borne vibration. The main effect of vibration is to reduce the useful life of buildings and other structures. Sharp and Jennings (1976) state that there are two types of damage to buildings which can be caused by vibration. 'Architectural damage' refers to the cracking of plaster and other brittle material, and 'structural damage' implies that the building itself is in danger. Banister and Button (1993) say that road freight transport poses a particular problem in historic urban areas, where buildings are particularly susceptible to damage from vibration.

The level of ground-borne vibration depends partly on the condition of the road (Ogden, 1992), so that it can be controlled by good road construction. Ground-borne vibration also depends on vehicle axle weights, suspension systems and tyre stiffness and speed (Armitage, 1980). Unfortunately, both road and vehicle conditions are not always particularly good in developing countries and this exacerbates the problem. Air-borne vibration, which is related partly to engine noise, is not easy to control, because, as Ogden (1992) says, and according to Department of Transport information, quietening the engine will not necessarily remove the problem of low frequency air-borne vibration. Button (1993) considers that, in general, vibration has effects on those living in houses close to transport infrastructure in terms of disrupting their sleep which in turn can have health implications as well as affecting their general enjoyment of life.

Road wear Heavy vehicles are the predominant cause of damage to road surface and structures (Plowden, 1985). In towns, underground services, such as gas, water, electricity, telephone, information cables and sewers can be damaged. Road wear caused by goods vehicles results from both gross weight and axle weight or loading. Following road tests carried out by the

American Association of State Highway Officials (AASHO) in 1958 to 1960, road damage has been calculated using the fourth power law. This means than an axle of six tonnes compared to an axle of five tonnes is $6^4:5^4$ or 1296:625, i.e. it does nearly twice as much damage. Environmentalists have argued that a fifth power would be more appropriate, in which case, the damage from the heavier axles would be even greater. Indeed, where road surfaces are weak, it can be argued that an even higher exponent should be used.

Because of the fourth power law, nearly all road damage can be attributed to lorries (Armitage, 1980). Many countries have differential taxes for goods vehicles to compensate for this. In the UK, the Vehicle Excise Duty (VED) increases with increasing vehicle weight so that, according to the DETR, HGVs (heavy goods vehicles) cover their road track costs through a combination of VED and fuel duty.

Social considerations - safety In Great Britain in 1996, around 3,600 people were killed and 48,000 were killed or seriously injured (DETR, 1997a). Britain, however, has one of the best road safety records in the world. Whereas Great Britain has 1.4 road deaths per 10,000 vehicles licensed, Morocco has 25.6, China 43.8 and Ethiopia a staggering 191.6 deaths (The Red Cross 1998). It is also noted that many developing countries do not even compile statistics on road accidents.

In the UK, HGV's are less likely than cars to be involved in an accident, but when they are involved, the accidents are more likely to be serious. Thus, in Great Britain, for every 100 million vehicle km, 0.3 car drivers are killed and 36 are injured. When a HGV is involved, 1.9 people are killed and 44 are injured (DETR, 1997b). Using data on accidents in the USA in 1989, Ogden (1992) found that about 75 per cent of persons killed in fatal crashes involving a heavy goods vehicle were not occupants of that vehicle. For medium-sized goods vehicles the corresponding figure was 73 per cent.

Valuing life is one of the most controversial elements of cost benefit analysis (and the method of cost benefit analysis used in the UK would be particularly inappropriate to developing countries, being based on income foregone). However, by any measurement, road accidents impose a great cost on society and need to be minimised.

Intrusion This problem relates to all transport rather than only road freight transport. According to Banister and Button (1993) problems of *visual* intrusion come from both transport infrastructure and the vehicles using it. They add that it is strictly the blocking out of light or pleasant views by transport activities. Armitage (1980) suggests that the main instances where lorries cause intrusion are 'on journeys through settlements using inadequate roads' or where they are in the wrong place, e.g. when HGVs are being used for deliveries in towns, or being parked on residential streets, or when depots are located in residential areas.

Congestion Congestion has a considerable effect on goods vehicle operating costs, either directly through its effect on productivity and fuel consumption, or indirectly through its effect on transport operations (Ogden, 1992). Button and Pearman (1981) point out that goods vehicles 'exacerbate congestion' in three main ways; causing a delay in a stream of traffic, due to their relatively poor acceleration; while moving into or out of a traffic stream; and while parking and loading or unloading. On the other hand, congestion may be seen as a lack of internal efficiency of transport operations rather than a form of environmental problem (Banister and Button, 1993). Concerning the delays caused by goods vehicles to other road users, Sharp (1992) says that it can be reduced by increasing the power to weight ratio of goods vehicles, so that they can accelerate more quickly.

According to Transport and Road Research Laboratory estimations for the effect of goods vehicles on congestion, the delay to other road users caused by heavy goods vehicles travelling on an urban road was in the range 0.2 - 1.0 minute per vehicle kilometre (Button and Pearman, 1981). In 1992, the Faculty of Freight of the Chartered Institute of Transport issued a report on congestion. The report includes the implications of congestion on cost, productivity, environment and also the social implications of congestion in Britain. These included increased household expenditure, higher travel costs of individuals, slower average speed, higher distribution costs, higher inventory levels and lower productivity.

Privatisation and externalities

Privatisation in a non-market economy should be seen as part of a wider process of transformation to a market-orientated economy, where the price mechanism is supposed to achieve the optimal resource allocation. In such an economy, the issue of externalities is an important one. In economic theory, the market is a meeting point where individuals maximise their benefits and firms maximise their profits. Given perfect competition, the pricing system will achieve the efficient distribution of all goods and services, and also of the production factors. The pricing system should include all relevant costs to achieve optimum resource utilisation by the market. If it does not, it will result in distortions of the same kind as that which results from subsidies (Kageson, 1993). Where externalities exist, the market is inevitably distorted.

In Egypt, it is unlikely that private road freight operators could be persuaded to cover their external costs. Certainly, the panellists in the Delphi exercise disagreed that under privatisation of the road freight industry, the operators should pay for the damage to the environment resulting from running their operations. This result is quite understandable, since awareness of road freight external costs appears to be low in Egypt. However, a review of the panel replies shows that for most of the panellists, the principle is acceptable, subject to gradual application. In the UK, although operators cover the road track costs, the Royal Commission on Environmental Pollution (1994) calculated that HGVs only covered between 49 per cent and 68 per cent of environmental and public costs and this did not include all environmental costs. The Egyptian Delphi panel disagreed that the current tax on fuel in Egypt was adequate to cover the social and environmental costs resulting from road freight operations. The panel considered, however, that the external cost of road freight operations was more than just air pollution and that consequently, there was a need for other types of taxes, for example on tyres.

The Delphi exercise suggested that making private road haulage pay for social and environmental costs would result in price increases in the short term, but that in the medium and long term, cost increases would be absorbed by the industry and prices would not be too high. The panel agreed that prices would increase in the short term but disagreed that the cost increases would be absorbed by the industry in the medium and long term, resulting in insignificant price rises in the long run.

Although operators need to be encouraged to cover their external costs, privatisation of the road freight transport industry need not necessarily lead to an *increase* in the external costs of road freight transport. It could well be argued that one of the major effects of privatisation, so long as it is accompanied by deregulation, should be to increase the efficiency of the industry. Given that many of the externalities discussed above (for instance, pollution, noise and vibration) are linked to vehicle use, more efficient use of vehicles through, for example, better scheduling or less empty running, could actually improve the situation. Additionally, many of the externalities discussed above are also linked to the maintenance of vehicles. Under privatisation, maintenance standards could improve as competition forces the use of more modern vehicles and more reliable schedules. The impression gained in the UK is that since privatisation, the stock of vehicles is newer and, generally, operators are more responsible in terms of safety and the environment.

Conclusions

This chapter has considered some of the external costs of road freight transport, particularly those pertaining to developing countries. A major issue relating to privatisation is that private operators impose costs on others for which they do not pay and this results in market distortions. Although this is probably not considered to be of prime importance in economies where the major goal of privatisation is to increase the efficiency of the economy, it is an issue which, nevertheless, needs to be considered.

Even in advanced economies, the issue of externalities causes a great deal of concern. The Rio and Kyoto summits have focused attention on issues such as global warming, and other effects such as acid rain and photochemical smog make everyday news. Vehicles probably do not cover their environmental costs in any country in the world, although steps are being taken to cover an ever-increasing proportion of such costs. The Delphi panellists in Egypt did not rule out gradual inclusion of such costs in goods vehicle tax, although hardly surprisingly, they did not consider that this should be done immediately.

8   Conclusions

Much of the world is currently going through, or has recently been through, processes of privatisation and deregulation of its industry. Encouraged by the collapse of the communist doctrine in many countries, market forces have not seen such popularity in centuries. The main focus of this book has been on the road freight industry which, although not usually the first industry in any country to be privatised, has often not been far behind. The main reason for this is probably that an efficient road freight industry is required to support the needs of an efficient manufacturing sector; it is pointless improving the efficiency of the manufacturing sector if the means of delivery of those goods does not exist or is slow and bureaucratic. In addition, with the widening of trade markets and increases in international trade volumes, the smooth transport of goods from ship, through ports and on to final destination is even more important. It is now widely believed, and has been proven in many individual studies, that privatisation improves efficiency.

A major reason for public sector control of road freight transport in the past has been the desire to ensure that 'fair' competition exists between road and rail. Without some form of control, it has been considered that road would have an unfair competitive advantage over rail. Most governments have a desire to ensure the future of the railways, both because of an inherent belief that rail is in some ways better (in part to do with the environment) and for strategic defence reasons. The most obvious way of exerting control over the road freight industry was to have it under government ownership. Nowadays, however, the strategic defence argument is no longer viewed as being of such great importance in many countries and other mechanisms of controlling the competition, for instance through fiscal measures, are viewed as being more effective. Indeed, the railways themselves have been privatised in some countries, such as the UK.

However, once it has been decided that road freight privatisation may be necessary, decisions as to how to privatise, how much to privatise, as well as over what time scale it should be done, must be taken. We have shown that there are many different methods of privatisation, including management or employee buy-outs, direct sale to a third party and public flotation. A large difference in approaches was shown to exist according to whether privatisation is to take place in an economy where private ownership is already the norm compared to instances where it is part of a wholesale restructuring reform. We have also discussed the difference between the gradualist and shock therapy approaches. From this, it must be apparent that there is no single established process of privatisation, and each has its advantages and disadvantages. The extent to which any method of privatisation dominates will partly depend on the characteristics of the economy itself.

Privatisation of the road freight industry on its own may have little impact on the industry. Deregulation is also of key importance as it is this which enables competition to take place. Private ownership without competition would be unlikely to result in improvements in efficiency; it would be more likely to lead to large increases in price and profits unless these were regulated in some way. Deregulation of the industry is, therefore, almost a prerequisite to privatisation. Deregulation need not imply a complete lack of regulation. Some form of regulation, for example to ensure the safe operation of vehicles, is obviously necessary. Deregulation often involves the imposition of 'quality' as opposed to 'quantity' constraints. Thus, entry into the industry is not directly controlled by government except insofar as it sets the minimum standards which goods vehicle operators must achieve before they are allowed to operate.

It is as a result of a combination of privatisation and deregulation that the logistics function has blossomed in many developed countries. The combination of the ability and the incentives to compete has meant that the hire and reward sector has taken over much of the work previously done in-house. Professionalism in the hire and reward sector has allowed trust between distributor and manufacturer to develop enabling manufacturers to concentrate on their core business. It is this that is required in developing countries.

Road freight transport is an industry in which there is often a proliferation of small businesses, essentially sole operators. This inevitably seems to mean that the bankruptcy rate is fairly high. One of the reasons for this appears to be that such operators have less time to maintain proper accounts, and the financial side of the operation is secondary to the operational side. There is also a problem, however, that competition can push down the rates charged for road freight to an artificially low level. This may be the case particularly where own account operators are allowed to compete for third party business, as they may cross-subsidise freight rates from other parts of their own business, such as production. The Egyptian Delphi panel argued that this was a reason for keeping a legal distinction between own account and hire and reward operators in Egypt, particularly immediately following privatisation, to allow the industry to settle down.

The existence of many small operators is no barrier to overall efficiency. There will probably always be a role for them in the road freight market. However, if the way to progress is through the development of a more integrated logistics approach, then large scale operators will also be required. Logistics and supply chain management require a great deal of investment. Apart from the vehicles, investment is required in warehouses, mechanical handling equipment, stock control systems, advanced communications networks and skilled manpower. It takes a large company to make this level of investment, and the privatisation process must take this into account.

One of the authors participated in a study tour of the distribution sector in the Czech Republic in 1995 when it was going through the process of road freight privatisation. One of the major problems encountered in the sector was that there were no freight transport companies large enough to cope with the demands of the privatised manufacturing industry. As a result, foreign road freight operators were entering the market and the rail network was being used for loads for which it was not really suited (e.g. chocolate in non air-conditioned wagons during the summer). The manufacturing sector was certainly suffering as a result.

Another major issue of privatisation is whether or not to maintain the same management and management structure. It could be argued that if a company under public sector ownership was not profitable, then without a change in management, there is no reason why it should be profitable under private sector ownership. Indeed, working under more capitalist conditions requires a complete change of culture for many companies and maintaining the same management and management structure might inhibit that transition. The counter-argument to this, however, is that with training, the right incentives and a super-imposed system of performance targets, existing managers (or at least some of them) may adapt to the new conditions fairly well. Additionally, without them (or some of them), the transition could be sabotaged. In a country where the prevailing culture is one of collective ownership, finding managers with the right skills and culture to replace existing ones may not be easy. In some instances, this problem has been tackled, not always successfully, by bringing in consultants and managers from overseas either to take over or to train indigenous staff.

Probably the major problem with privatisation of road freight in Egypt is over-manning. Many of the public sector road freight companies are vastly overstaffed as a way of maintaining full employment. The Delphi panel agreed that much of the labour force would have to be shed if road freight privatisation took place, but without unemployment benefit, this could threaten the political stability of the country. They were not in favour of using the proceeds of the sale of the companies to help finance the expansion of the small business sector to absorb some of the unemployed. In the longer term, some of those made unemployed may be re-employed as the transport and other sectors grow through efficiency. In the short term, however, this is of no comfort to those who would be made unemployed. There is no easy way around this problem. Providing a system of social security may be the only partial solution, but this would cost the Egyptian government substantial funds which it does not have.

In the UK, the state sector road freight industry was privatised through a management/employee buy-out in the early 1980s. As this was the first of its kind in the UK, the process took some years to accomplish since laws had to be changed to allow it to take place. Money was raised through an employee loan scheme despite initial union objections and no real tradition of share ownership amongst the ordinary working people of the UK. Much of the management remained unchanged and their involvement and enthusiasm for the buy-out provided much of the impetus behind it. It was the managers who both persuaded employees to invest in the buy-out and steered it through the subsequent years. Might this then be a good example for other countries to adopt?

One of the major differences between the UK and Egypt is that the UK has a history of a successful stock market and well established financial institutions. When all is said and done, it was the commercial banks in the UK which agreed to back the buy-out and put up the majority of the funding. Although Egypt has a stock exchange, it is not heavily used and has a history of instability. Confidence of the Egyptian population in the financial organisations is not particularly high. Whilst there is no doubt that there is available finance in Egypt (and this was certainly borne out by the Delphi exercise), the desire to invest in the Egyptian market may not be so great. Whether the managers in Egypt would have the ability or desire to spearhead the buy-out is another debatable issue. However, the biggest barrier would be the over-manning problem, as discussed above. Unless a substantial amount of labour could be shed, with no subsequent ill-effect on the economy as a whole, the prospects for the freight companies under privatisation do not look great, particularly for the immediate future. It is certainly a risk that neither the management nor the employees would probably want to take.

References

Abdallah A. and Brown M. (1988), 'The Economy', in Harris L. (ed.), *Egypt: Internal Challenges and Regional Stability*, Chatham House Paper No. 39, Routledge and Kegan Paul: London.

Abdel-Fattah N. (1988), *The Relationship between the Population Component in the National Development Plans and the National Population Policy in Egypt*, MSc Thesis, Al-Azhar University: Cairo.

Abu Shair, O.J.A. (1997), *Privatization and Development*, Macmillan: Basingstoke.

Adam, J. (1995), 'The transition to a market economy in Hungary', *Europe-Asia Studies*, Vol. 47, No. 6, pp. 989-1006.

Adam Smith Institute (1986), *Privatisation Worldwide*, Adam Smith Institute: London.

Adrangi, B., Chow, G. and Raffiee, K. (1995), 'Analysis of the deregulation of the US Trucking Industry', *Journal of Transport Economics and Policy*, Vol. 29, No. 3, pp. 233-246.

Africa Review (1995), World of Information, Saffron Walden.

Ajami, F. (1995), 'The sorrows of Egypt', *Foreign Affairs*, Vol. 74, No. 5, pp. 72-88.

Al-Ahram (1991), *IMF negotiations concluded*, 20 June, p. 1.

Al-Ahram (1994), *Reduce interest rate on loans for workers' shares*, 10 August, p. 7.

Al-Ahram (1996), *State sector companies' debts, how much?*, 8 April, p. 10.

Al-Mossawer (1994), *Press conference, Minister of the Businesses Sector talks about the task*, 30 December, pp. 28-33.

Alchian, A. and Demsetz, H. (1972), 'Production, information costs and economic organization', *American Economic Review*, No. 62, pp. 777-795.

Allsopp, C. (1989), 'The macro-economic role of the state', in Helm, D. (ed.), *The Economic Borders of the State*, Oxford University Press: Oxford.

Andreff, W. (1992), 'French privatisation techniques and experience', in Targetti, F. (ed.), *Privatisation in Europe, West and East Experiences*, Dartmouth: Aldershot.

Armitage, A. (1980), *Report of the Inquiry into Lorries, People and the Environment*, HMSO: London.

Aylen, J. (1987), 'Privatisation in Developing Countries', *Lloyds Bank Review*, No. 163, January, pp. 15-30.

Bamford, C. (1995), *Transport Economics*, Heinemann Educational: Oxford.

Banister, D. and Button, K.J. (ed.) (1993), *Transport, the Environment and Sustainable Development*, E. & F.N. Spon: London.

Banker (1990), 'It is a long road', *Banker*, Vol. 140, No. 773, pp. 62-64.

Baum, H. (1991), *The Role of Government in a Deregulated Transport Market*, Economic Research Centre: Paris.

Baumol, W.J. and Oates, W.E. (1988), *The Theory of Environmental Policy*, Cambridge University Press: Cambridge.

Beesley, M. and Littlechild, S. (1988), 'Privatisation, principles, problems and priorities', in Johnson, C. (ed.), *Privatisation and Ownership*, Lloyds Bank Annual Review, No. 1, pp. 11-29.

Beinin, J. (1989), 'Labour, capital and the state in Nasserist Egypt', *International Journal of Middle East Studies*, Vol. 21, No. 1, pp. 71-90.

Benson, D. (1992), *Elements of Road Transport Management*, Croner: Kingston Upon Thames.

Berend, T.I. and Ranki, G. (1985), *The Hungarian Economy in The Twentieth Century*, Croom Helm: London.

Biggs, C. and Benjamin, D. (1989), *Management Accounting Techniques: an Integrated Approach*, Heineman Professional: Oxford.

Bishop, M. and Kay, J. (1988), *Does Privatisation Work*, London Business School: London.

Bleaney, M. (1994), 'Economic liberalisation in Eastern Europe: problems and prospects', *World Economy*, Vol. 17, No. 4, pp. 497-507.

Boardman, A. and Vining, A. (1989), 'Ownership and performance in competitive environment', *Journal of Law and Economics*, Vol. 32, No. 1, pp. 1-33.

Bogetic, Z. (1993), 'The role of employee ownership in privatisation of state enterprises in Eastern and Central Europe', *Europe-Asia Studies*, Vol. 45, No. 3, pp. 463-482.

Bolton, P. and Roland, G. (1992), 'Privatisation policies in Central and Eastern Europe', *Economic Policy*, Vol. 7, No. 15, pp. 275-310.

Bos, D. (1986), *Public Enterprise Economics; Theory and Practice*, North-Holland: Amsterdam.

Bos, D. (1993), 'Privatisation in Europe: a comparison of approaches', *Oxford Review of Economic Policy*, Vol. 9, No. 1, pp. 95-110.

Bos, D. and Nett, L. (1991), 'Employee share ownership and privatisation', *Economic Journal*, Vol. 101, No. 407, pp. 966-969.

Bouin, O. and Michalet, CH-A. (1991), *Rebalancing the Public and Private Sectors: Developing Country Experience*, OECD: Paris.

Bradley, K. and Nejad, A. (1989), *Managing Owners: The National Freight Consortium in Perspective*, Cambridge University Press: Cambridge.

Budapest Sun (1995), *EU trucking laws to benefit big outfits*, 21 May, pp. 1-2.

Button, K.J. (1993), *Transport Economics*, Edward Elgar: Aldershot.

Button, K.J. (1993), *Transport, the Environment and Economic Policy*, Edward Elgar: Aldershot.

Button, K.J. and Chow, G. (1983), 'Road haulage deregulation: a comparison of the Canadian, British and American approaches', *Transport Reviews*, Vol. 3, No. 3, pp. 237-264.

Button, K.J. and Pearman, A.D. (1981), *The Economics of Urban Freight Transport*, Macmillan: London.

CAPMAS (1992), *Statistical Year Book 1991*, Cairo.

Carlin, W. and Mayer, C. (1992), 'Restructuring enterprises in Eastern Europe', *Economic Policy*, Vol. 7, No. 15, pp. 311-352.

Carr, D. (1990), 'The possibility of rapid adjustment to severe budget-deficit and other economic problems in Egypt', *Journal of Developing Areas*, Vol. 24, No. 2, pp. 225-246.

Central Bank of Egypt (1990), *Annual Economic Review*.

Central Bank of Egypt (1992), *Annual Economic Review*.

Central Bank of Egypt (1993), *Quarterly Economic Review*, Vol. 33, No. 1.

Central Bank of Egypt (1993b), *Quarterly Economic Review*, Vol. 33, No. 4.

Central Bank of Egypt (1994), *Annual Economic Review*.

Central Bank of Egypt (1995), *Quarterly Economic Review*, Vol. 35, No. 3.

Chan, A. (1987), *Management Accounting - Decision Making*, Butterworth: London.

Chikan, A. (1996), 'Consequences of economic transition on logistics: the case of Hungary', *International Journal of Physical Distribution and Logistics Management*, Vol. 26, No. 1, pp. 40-48.

Christopher, M. (1992), *Logistics and Supply Chain Management*, Pitman Publishing: London.

Clague, C. and Rausser, G.C. (1992), *The Emergence of Market Economics in Eastern Europe*, Blackwell: Oxford.

Clementi, D. (1985), 'The experience of the United Kingdom', *Asian Development Bank Privatisation*, pp. 167-182.

Coase, R. (1960), 'The problem of social cost', *Journal of Law and Economics*, Vol. 3, October, pp. 1-44.

Committee of Inquiry into Operators' Licensing (1979), Chairman: Christopher Foster, *Road Haulage Operator's Licensing*, HMSO: London.

Committee on the Problem of Noise (1963), Chairman: Sir Alan Wilson, *Cmnd 2056*, HMSO: London.

Cooper, J. (ed.) (1993), *Strategy Planning in Logistics and Transportation*, Kogan Page: London.

Cone, J.D. and Hayes, S. (1984), *Environmental Problems: Behavioural Solutions*, Cambridge University Press: Cambridge.

Coyle, J.J., Bardi, E.J., and Langley, C.J., (1996), *The Management of Business Logistics* (6th edition), West Publishing: St. Paul, MN.

Cullinane, S.L. and Cullinane, K.P.B. (1995), 'Increasing car ownership and use in Egypt: the straw that breaks the camel's back?', *International Journal of Transport Economics*, Vol. 22, No. 1, pp. 35-63.

Davies, D. (1971), 'The efficiency of public versus private firms, the case of Australia's two airlines', *Journal of Law and Economics*, Vol. 14, No. 1, pp. 149-165.

Demsetz, H. (1964), 'The exchange and enforcement of property rights', *Journal of Law and Economics*, October, pp. 11-26.

DETR (1997a), *Transport Statistics, Great Britain*, TSO: London.

DETR (1997b), *Road Accidents Great Britain: 1996, The Casualty Report*, TSO: London.

Dietz, F. and Stratten, J. (1992), 'Rethinking environmental economics; missing links between economic theory and environmental policy', *Journal of Economic Issues*, Vol. 26, No. 1, pp. 27-52.

Dodgson, J.S. and Topham, N. (1988), *Bus Deregulation and Privatisation: an International Perspective*, Avebury: Aldershot.

Domberger, S. and Piggott, J. (1994), 'Privatisation Policies and Public Enterprise', in Bishop, M. *et al* (eds.), *Privatisation and Economic Performance*, Oxford University Press: Oxford.

Egyptian American Company for Road Freight (1992), *Annual Report 1991*, Alexandria.

Egyptian Railways Authority (1993), *Statistical Year Book 1992*, Cairo.

El-Mazawy, A. and Lashin, A. (1994), *Changes in the road freight market in Egypt*, Report presented to Minister of the State Sector, Cairo.

Euromoney (1990), 'Back-Door Route to Privatisation', September, pp. 42-45.

Euromoney (1994), 'Planned Privatisation in Egypt', December, p. 58.

Euromoney (1994), 'Privatisation in Hungary', September, pp. 188-190.

Euromoney (1995), 'Only the exit doors are open', April, p. 80.

Euromoney (1996), 'Social Cost of Privatisation', January, p. 111.

Europe Review (1994), 'World of Information', Saffron Walden.

Ferguson, P. (1992), 'Privatisation options for Eastern Europe: the irrelevance of Western experience', *World Economy*, Vol. 15, No. 4, pp. 487-504.

Ferner, A. and Colling, T. (1991), 'Privatisation, regulation and industrial relations', *British Journal of Industrial Relations*, Vol. 29, No. 3, pp. 391-409.

Filatotchey, I., Buck, T. and Wright, M. (1992), 'Privatisation and entrepreneurship in the break-up of the USSR', *World Economy*, Vol. 15, No. 4, pp. 505-524.

Frydman, R. (1993) (main author), *The Privatisation Process in Central Europe*, Central Europe University: London.

Gazale, L. (1994), 'Morocco fuels incentives for foreign investment', *Arab World Online: Tradeline*, 23 September.

General Association for Road Freight Transport (1988), *Annual Report 1987*, Cairo.

General Association for Road Freight Transport (1992), *Annual Report 1991*, Cairo.

General Authority for Roads and Bridges (1994), *Road Length in Egypt*, Cairo.

Ghosh, S. (1994), 'Privatisation', *Journal of General Management*, Vol. 20, No. 1, pp. 72-81.

Gillespie, K. and Stoever, W. (1988), 'Investment Promotion in Sadat's Egypt, Lessons for Less-Developed Countries', *Journal of Arab Affairs*, Vol. 7, No. 1, pp. 19-48.

Gomulka, S. (1994), 'Economic and political constraints during transition', *Europe-Asia Studies*, Vol. 46, No. 1, pp. 89-106.

Goodwin, P.B., Hallett, S.L., Kenny, F. and Stokes, G. (1991), *Transport: the New Realism*, Report to the Rees Jeffrey's Road Fund.

Grosfeld, I. (1991), 'Privatisation of the state enterprises in Eastern Europe', *East European Politics and Societies*, Vol. 5, No. 1, pp. 142-161.

Guria, J. (1989), 'An assessment of the effects of road freight transport regulation in developing countries', *International Journal of Transport Economics*, Vol. 16, No. 3, pp. 237-262.

Hallett, S. and Gray, R. (1987), 'The operating costs of heavy lorries', *Management Research News*, Vol. 10, No. 3, pp. 14-16.

Haq, G. (1997), *Towards Sustainable Transport Planning*, Avebury: Aldershot.

Hare, P.G., Radice, H.K. and Swain, N. (1981), *Hungary, A Decade of Economic Reform*, Allen and Unwin: London.

Hare, P.G. and Revesz, T. (1992), 'Hungary's transition to the market', *Economic Policy*, Vol. 7, No. 14, pp. 227-264.

Haritos, Z. (1987), 'Public transport enterprises in transition', *Transportation*, Vol. 14, No. 3, pp. 193-207.

Harris, L.C. (ed.) (1988), *Egypt: Internal Challenges and Regional Stability*, Routledge and Kegan Paul: London.

Harris, N.G. and Godward, E. (1997), *The Privatisation of BR*, The Railway Consultancy Press: London.

Held, C.C. (1989), *Middle East Patterns: Places, Peoples and Politics*, Westview Press: Boulder, Col.

Helm, D. (1986), 'The Economic Borders of The State', *Oxford Review of Economic Policy*, Vol. 2, No. 2, pp. 1-24.

Helm, D. (1989), 'The Economic Borders of The State', in Helm, D. (ed.), *The Economic Borders of The State*, Oxford University: Oxford.

Helm, D. and Pearce, D. (1990), 'Assessment: economic policy towards the environment', *Oxford Review of Economic Policy*, Vol. 6, No. 1, pp. 1-16.

Himanen, V., Nijkamp, P. and Padjen, J. (1992), 'Environmental quality and transport policy in Europe', *Transportation Research*, Vol. 26A, No. 2, pp. 147-157.

Holding Company for Transport (1993), *Annual Report 1992*, Cairo.

Hoppe, C.W. (1980), 'Deregulation gives traffic managers entrepreneurial options', *Traffic World*, February, p. 23.

Hopwood, D. (1982), *Egypt,Politics and Society*, Allen and Unwin: London.

Houghton, J. (1994), *Global Warming: The Complete Briefing*, Lion: Oxford.

Husain, A. and Sahay, R. (1992), 'Does Sequencing of Privatisation Matter in Reforming Planned Economies?', in *IMF Staff Papers*, Vol. 39, No. 4, pp. 801-824.

Hussey, R. (1989), *Cost and Management Accounting*, Macmillan: Basingstoke.

Hyclak, T. and King, A. (1994), 'The privatisation experience in Eastern Europe', *World Economy*, Vol. 17, No. 4, pp. 529-550.

Ismailia National Company for Road Haulage (1992), *Annual Report* 1991, Ismailia.

Jiyad, A. (1995), 'The social balance sheet of privatisation in the Arab countries', The Third Nordic Conference on Middle Eastern Studies, Finland, June.

Kageson, P. (1993), *Getting the Prices Right*, The European Federation for Transport and Environment.

Kapp, W. (1972), 'On the Nature and Significance of Social Costs', in Staaf, R.J. and Tannian, F. (eds.), *Externalities, Theoretical Dimensions of Political Economy*, Dunellen: New York.

Karsai, J. and Wright, M. (1994), 'Accountability, governance and finance in Hungarian buy-outs', *Europe Asia Studies*, Vol. 46, No. 6, pp. 997-1016.

Kay, J. and Thompson, P. (1986), 'Privatisation: a policy in search of a rationale', *Economic Journal*, No. 96, pp. 18-32.

Kent, V. (1993), *Investing in Egypt:A Guide to the Current Economic Climate*, Committee for Middle East Trade: London.

Key Note Report (1984), *Road Haulage*, Key Note: London.

Key Note Report (1992), *Road Haulage: a Market Sector Overview*, Key Note: Hampton.

Key Note Report (1996), *Road Haulage*, Key Note: Hampton.

Laurie, S. (1989), 'Egypt: tiptoeing towards reform', *Banker*, Vol. 139, No. 761, pp. 147-153.

Lawson, C. (1994), 'The theory of state-owned enterprises in market economies', *Journal of Economic Surveys*, Vol. 8, No. 3, pp. 283-309.

Letwin, O. (1988), *Privatising the World*, Cassell: London.

Lieberman, I.W. (1994), 'Privatisation in Latin America and Eastern Europe in the context of political and economic reform', *World Economy*, Vol. 17, No. 4, pp. 551-575.

Lindsay, M. (1992), *Developing Capital Market in Eastern Europe*, Printer Publishers: London.

Liu, Z. (1995), 'The comparative performance of public and private enterprises: the case of British ports', *Journal of Transport Economics and Policy*, Vol. 29, No. 3, pp. 263-274.

Lloyds Bank (1986), *Egypt,Economic Report*.

Lloyds Bank (1986), *Hungary,Economic Report*.

Lloyds Bank (1988), *Privatisation and Ownership*, Printer Publishers: London.

Lloyd's List (1997a), 'Everything up for sale', 28 November, p. 8.

Lloyd's List (1997b), 'Egytrans in position to gain from trend to liberalisation, 28 November, p. 9.

Lloyd's List (1998), 'Companies set to seize share of liberalised business', 8 January, p. 3.

Lofgren, H. (1993), 'Economic policy in Egypt, a breakdown in reform resistance', *International Journal of Middle East Studies*, Vol. 25, No. 3, pp. 407-429.

Lowe, D. (1983), *Goods Vehicles Costing and Pricing Handbook (3rd edition)*, Kogan Page: London.

Lowe, D. (1989), *Goods Vehicles Costing and Pricing Handbook (4th edition)*, Kogan Page: London.

Lowe, D. (1991), *A Study Manual of Professional Competence in Road Transport Management*, Kogan Page: London.

Mackett, R. (1992), 'Transport planning and operation in a changing economic and political environment: the case of Hungary', *Transport Reviews*, Vol. 12, No. 1, pp. 77-96.

Mahjoub, A. (ed.) (1990), *Adjustment or Delinking? The African Experience*, United Nations University Press: London.

Maltby, D. and White, H.P. (1982), *Transport in the United Kingdom*, Macmillan: London.

Mayer, C. (1989), 'Public Ownership, Concepts and Applications', in Helm, D. (ed.), *The Economic Borders of the State*, Oxford University Press: Oxford.

McClave, et al. (1986), 'Motor carrier deregulation, the Florida experiment', *The Review of Economics and Statistics*, Vol. 68, No. 3, pp. 159-164.

McDougall, R. (1988), 'Back to the good old basics', *Banker*, Vol. 138, No. 749, pp. 33-39.

McLachlan, S. (1983), *The National Freight Buy-Out*, Macmillan: London.

Middle East Review (1986), 'World of Information', Saffron Walden.

Middle East Review (1992), 'World of Information', Saffron Walden.

Middle East Review (1996), 'World of Information', Saffron Walden.

Minalan, T. (1998), 'Own, lease or outsource? You'll soon need to choose', *Purchasing On-line*, 26 March.

Ministry of Transport (1993), *Study of the National Transport System in Egypt*, unpublished, Cairo.

Mizsei, K. (1992), 'Privatisation in Eastern Europe: a comparative study of Poland and Hungary', *Soviet Studies*, Vol. 44, No. 2, pp. 283-296.

Mizsei, K. (1993), 'Hungary: gradualism needs a strategy', in Portes, R. (ed.), *Economic Transformation in Central Europe*, Centre for Economic Policy Research: London.

Molyneux, R. and Thompson, D. (1987), 'Nationalised industry performance: still third-rate?', *Fiscal Studies*, Vol. 8, No. 1, pp. 48-82.

Muller, G. (1995), *Intermodal Freight Transportation (3rd edition)*, Eno Transportation Foundation: Lansdowne VA.

Mullineux, A. (1992), 'Privatisation and financial structure in Eastern and Central European Countries', *National Westminster Bank Quarterly Review*, May, pp. 12-25.

Murray, N. (1994), *The Development of Supply Chain Management in Hungary*, MPhil Thesis, University of Huddersfield: Huddersfield.

Myant, M. (1993), 'Problems of transition in Eastern Europe', *British Review of Economic Issues*, Vol. 15, No. 37, pp. 9-32.

Narkiewicz, O.A. (1986), *Eastern Europe 1968-1984*, Croom Helm: London.

National Bank of Egypt (1992), *Quarterly Economic Review*, Vol. 45, No. 2.

National Bank of Egypt (1992b), *Quarterly Economic Review*, Vol. 45, No. 3.

National Bank of Egypt (1993), *Quarterly Economic Review*, Vol. 46, No. 1.

National Bank of Egypt (1995), *Quarterly Economic Review*, Vol. 48, No. 3.

Nejad, A. (1986), *The Employee Buy-Out of the National Freight Consortium*, Partnership Research: London.

OECD (1990), *Competition Policy and the Deregulation of Road Transport*, Organisation for Economic Co-operation and Development: Paris.

OECD (1995), *Mass Privatisation: an Initial Assessment*, Organisation for Economic Co-operation and Development: Paris.

Official Journal (1991), 19 June, Egypt.

Official Journal (1992), 10 June, Egypt.

Ogden, K.W. (1992), *Urban Goods Movement: a Guide to Policy and Planning*, Ashgate: Aldershot.

Parker, D. (1994), 'International aspects of privatisation', *British Review of Economic Issues*, Vol. 16, No. 38, pp. 1-32.

Pirie, M. (1985), 'Privatisation Benefits Everyone', *Institute of Public Affairs Review*, Summer.

Plowden, S. (1985), *Transport Reform: Changing to Rules*, Policy Studies Institute: London.

Port Said National Company for Freight Transport (1992), *Annual Report 1991*, Cairo.

Potter, S. (1997), *Vital Travel Statistics*, Landor: London.

Practical Financial Management (1987), 'Costing', *Practical Financial Management*, Vol. 25, No. 5, pp. 42-47.

Price Commission (1977), *The Road Haulage Industry*, HMSO: London.

Puxty, J. and Dodds, C. (1988), *Financial Management: Method and Meaning*, VNR International: London.

Ramanadham, V.V. (1991), 'The Economics of Public Enterprise', Routledge: London.

Ratcliffe, B. (1987), *Economy and Efficiency in Transport and Distribution*, Kogan Page: London.

Richardson, J.J. (ed.) (1990), *Privatisation and Deregulation in Canada and Britain*, Dartmouth: Aldershot.

Riecke, W. and Antal, L. (1993), 'Hungary: Sound Money, Fiscal Problems', in Portes, R. (ed.), *Economic Transformation in Central Europe*, Centre for Economic Policy Research: London.

Roe, M. (1992), *East European International Road Freight Haulage*, Avebury: Aldershot.

Rothengatter, W. (1994), 'Do external benefits compensate for external costs of transport?', *Transportation Research*, Vol. 28A, No. 4, pp. 321-328.

Royal Commission on Environmental Pollution (1994), *18th Report, Transport and the Environment, Cm2674*, HMSO: London.

Sabry, E. (1969), *State Sector: Theoretical and Empirical Issues*, Dar El-Maaref: Cairo.

Sachs, J. and Woo, T. (1994), 'Experiences in the transition to a market economy', *Journal of Comparative Economics*, Vol. 18, No. 2, pp. 271-275.

Shackleton, J. (1984), 'Privatisation: the case examined', *National Westminster Bank Quarterly Review*, May, pp. 59-73.

Sharp, C. and Jennings, T. (1976), *Transport and the Environment*, Leicester University Press: Leicester.

Shaw, H. (1991), *Finance in Organisations*, Elm Publications: Huntingdon.

Short, H. (1994), 'Ownership, control, financial structure and the performance of firms', *Journal of Economic Surveys*, Vol. 8, No. 3, pp. 203-249.

State Sector Information Centre (1995), *Financial Results of the Transport Companies*, Cairo.

Stevens, B. (1992), 'Prospects for privatisation in OECD Countries', *National Westminster Bank Quarterly Review*, August, pp. 2-22.

Study of the National Transport System in Egypt (1993), Draft Version, Cairo, (unpublished).

Stumpenhorst, R. (1992), *Pollution in Cairo, report by the German Embassy in Cairo, Ref. 106-104 SV/9*, Department 106, Federal Foreign Office: Bonn.

Talley, W.K. (1988), *Transport Carrier Costing*, Gordon and Breach: London.

The Red Cross (1998), *World Disasters Report*, Oxford University Press: Oxford.

Thompson, P. (1990), *Sharing the Success - The Story of NFC*, Collins: London.

Timewell, S. (1991), 'Egypt: one more final chance', *Banker*, Vol. 141, No. 785, pp. 40-48.

Todaro, M.P. (1994), *Economic Development*, Longman: New York.

Transport Retort (1993), May.

UN-ESCWA (1994), *State Sector Road Freight in Egypt*, March, Cairo.

United Nations Development Programme (1996), *Human Development Report*, Oxford University Press: Oxford.

United Nations Economic Commission for Europe (1992), *Economic Reforms in the European Centrally Planned Economies*, United Nations: New York.

United Nations Economic Commission for Europe (1996), *Annual Bulletin of Transport Statistics for Europe and North America*, United Nations: New York.

United Nations Industrial Development Organisation (1979), *The Public Sector and Industrial Development*, Vienna.

Verhoef, E. (1994), 'External effects and social costs of road transport', *Transportation Research*, Vol. 28A, No. 4, pp. 273-287.

Welfens, P. (1992), *Market-Oriented Systemic Transformation in Eastern Europe*, Springer: Berlin.

Williamson, K., Singer, M. and Bloomberg, D. (1985), 'The impact of regulatory reform on US for-hire freight transportation: carriers' perspective', *Transportation Journal*, Vol. 24, No. 4, pp. 28-51.

Williamson, K., Singer, M. and Peterson, R. (1983), 'The impact of regulatory reform on US for-hire freight transportation: the users' perspective', *Transportation Journal*, Vol. 22, No. 4, pp. 27-54.

Wilson, P. (1987), 'Fleet Costing', *Management Research News*, Vol. 10, No. 3, pp. 17-18.

Wiltshire, K. (1987), *Privatisation: the British Experience*, Longman Cheshire: Melbourne.

Winston, C. (1985), 'Conceptual developments in the economics of transportation: an interpretative survey', *Journal of Economic Literature*, Vol. 23, No. 1, pp. 57-94.

Winston, C. et al. (1990), *The Economic Effects of Surface Freight Deregulation*, The Brookings Institution: Washington DC.

Wistrich, E. (1983), *The Politics of Transport*, Longman: London.

Worcester, D. (1972), 'Pecuniary and Technological Externality', in Staaf, R.J. and Tannian, F. (eds.), *Externalities, Theoretical Dimensions of Political Economy*, Dunellen: New York.

World Bank (1982), 'The Hungarian Economic Reform', *Working Paper No. 506*, February, Washington DC.

World Bank (1990), *World Development Report*, Oxford University Press: New York.

World Bank (1994), *World Development Report*, Oxford University Press: New York.

World Bank (1994), *World Development Report 1994: Infrastructure for Development*, Oxford University Press: New York.

Wright, M. et al. (1994), 'Management Buy-outs and Privatisation', in Bishop, M. et al. (eds.), *Privatisation and Economic Performance*, Oxford University Press: Oxford.

Yarrow, G. (1986), 'Privatisation in theory and practice', *Economic Policy*, Vol. 1, No. 2, pp. 323-378.

Ying, J. (1990), 'The inefficiency of regulating a competitive industry: productivity gains in trucking following reform', *Review of Economics and Statistics*, Vol. 72, No. 2, pp. 191-201.

Appendix

Delphi study of the Egyptian road freight industry

Introduction

The Delphi technique has been defined by Linstone and Turoff (1975) as a method for structuring a group communication process. In other words, it allows a group of individuals, usually experts, to deal with a complex problem in a structured way. In the Egyptian road freight study the Delphi technique consisted of two rounds of questions directed at a panel of experts. The experts did not meet each other, and their responses to the first round questionnaire formulated the second questionnaire for the second round. The objective was to explore the views of the experts sufficiently to obtain their collective viewpoint on significant issues regarding the privatisation of the Egyptian road freight industry. The Delphi approach was considered suitable for Egypt where there is not a tradition of widespread industry-based research.

The main five issues of privatisation of the Egyptian road freight industry were identified based on preliminary investigation. They are:

- impact of privatisation on the road freight industry
- the role of freight management under privatisation
- the best method of achieving privatisation of the state sector road freight companies
- macroeconomic problems facing privatisation of the state sector road freight companies
- the external costs of road freight under privatisation.

Each of these issues leads to a set of assumptions, which, in turn, lead to a set of statements, which form the basis for the Delphi study.

Issues presented to the panel of experts

Issue 1

Impact of privatisation on the road freight industry.

Assumption 1.1 The productivity of the state sector enterprises is lower than that of the private sector, and privatisation leads to improved performance through the ability to transfer ownership.

Statements:
- Under the privatisation of road haulage, the size of the state sector should be minimised as much as possible.

- Privatisation will inevitably create a more efficient, flexible and dynamic road freight industry.

- By privatising the road freight industry, there will be an opportunity to release more government money for spending on transport infrastructure (especially roads).

- Privatisation should not mean withdrawing subsidies totally from the transport industry. Some parts of the transport system need to be supported.

Assumption 1.2 The effect of privatisation, as a means of increasing efficiency, depends on the introduction of competition, which could be introduced by deregulation. Evidence suggests that deregulation of the road freight industry results in reduced rates, costs, and improved services.

Statements:
- Competition is the most important element for a high quality road freight industry.

- Road freight customers will benefit from privatising the industry in terms of lower charges.

- Road freight customers will benefit from privatising the industry in terms of a better quality of service.

Assumption 1.3 Deregulation may result in excessive competition. Evidence suggests that, following deregulation, rates fall sharply as a result of excessive competition. It would suggest that a form of regulating competition is needed to save the operators' profitability, which could applied by the government or through self-regulation.

Statements:

- Negative results might result from excessive competition in the transport sector. Therefore, a form of regulation of competition should be applied by the government to save the operators' profitability.

- It is not necessary to regulate competition in road freight through the government, because the freight operators can do it voluntarily through self-regulation.

- A privatised, deregulated road haulage industry requires a legal distinction to be made by the government between own account operators and professional operators.

Issue 2

Role of freight management under privatisation.

Assumption 2.1 The transfer to private ownership may result in improved cost efficiency by sharpening managerial incentives. Privatisation may also entail the adoption of management objectives that respond to the wish of the shareholders, which is maximising profits.

Statements:

- Under privatisation, identifying areas where cost reduction could be made is the main task for road freight management.

- To maximise profits should be the main objective for road freight management under privatisation.

Issue 3

Best method of achieving privatisation of the road freight industry.

Assumption 3.1 The privatisation of the state sector road freight companies presents different options. One approach is to dissolve the companies and sell off their assets. Another approach is to privatise them as a large entities, or to privatise the management only.

Statements:

- A good way to achieve privatisation of the road haulage industry is to dissolve the existing companies and sell off all their assets.

- A good way to achieve privatisation of the road haulage industry is to sell off the companies, in their existing form, through tenders.

- A good way to achieve privatisation of the road haulage industry is to transfer the companies' assets to shares, which could be sold through the stock exchange.

- A good way to achieve privatisation of the road haulage industry is to transfer the companies' assets to shares, using part of these shares to encourage early and voluntary retirement of the employees and use the remaining shares as workers' shares.

- Different state sector road haulage companies require different forms of privatisation (e.g. privatising management only or privatising both management and ownership).

- A wider base of popular capitalism is an important element to achieve successful privatisation of the road haulage industry, and requires low priced shares.

Issue 4

Macroeconomic problems facing privatisation of the road freight industry.

Assumption 4.1 The problem of capital required to finance privatisation, due to the lack of domestic savings, could be overcome by allowing foreign capital to participate in the privatisation process. The fear of foreign control over industries could be overcome by determining the maximum percentage of foreign capital in the companies, or by using employee buy-outs.

Statements:
- The lack of available capital is one of the most important problems facing the privatisation process of the road freight industry in developing countries.

- The problem of the lack of available capital could be avoided by allowing foreign capital to buy the assets of the state sector (particularly road haulage).

- Foreign control over the road freight industry will result if foreign capital is allowed to buy state assets in the road freight industry.

- The problem of foreign capital control over the road freight industry could be avoided by determining a maximum percentage for the capital owned by a foreigner in the road haulage companies.

- To avoid the problem of foreign capital control over the road freight industry, the government should sell the shares of the state-owned road haulage companies to their existing employees with interest free credit.

Assumption 4.2 The problem of increased unemployment arises from the fact that economies in transition operate with excess labour, due to the type of technology used and to achieve the social objective of full employment of the work force. On the other hand, the government ability to pay for the dismissed employees, or re-training them, or transferring them to other sectors is limited. The revenue from privatisation could be employed to encourage new small businesses.

Statements:
- Increased unemployment is one of the most important problems facing the privatisation of the road freight industry.

- The ability of the government to pay for dismissed employees (as a result of privatisation), or re-training them, or transferring them to other activities is one of the problems facing the privatisation processes.

- The problem of increased unemployment could be overcome by employing revenue from selling state sector road haulage companies to encourage new small road haulage businesses.

Issue 5

The external cost of road freight under privatisation.

Assumption 5.1 When applying the market economy model and price system, the operators should pay for the externalities. It might result in price increases, but through cost reductions, any cost increase would be absorbed by the industry, and as a result the price will not be too high.

Statements:
- Under privatisation, road freight operators should pay for the damage to the environment resulting from running their operations.

- A tax on fuel is adequate to cover the social and environmental costs resulting from road freight operations.

- Making private road haulage pay for social and environment costs will result in price increases in the short term.

- In the medium and long terms, cost increases, resulting from private road haulage paying for social and environment costs, will be absorbed by the industry and prices will not be too high.

It is possible to show the conceptual structure of the research by means of two diagrams. Appendix Figure 1 shows how road freight companies may be placed within a privatising economy. Appendix Figure 2 presents a diagrammatic version of the issues and assumptions previously introduced.

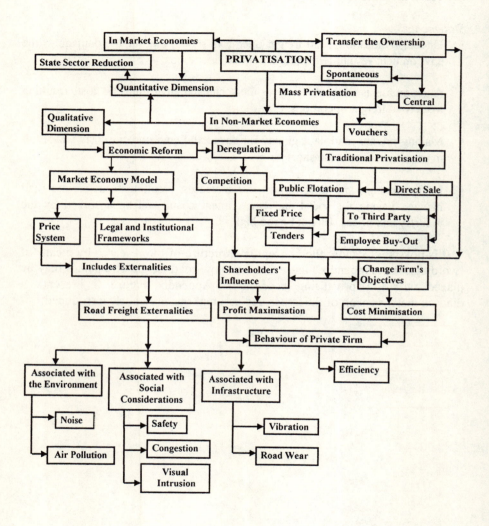

Appendix Figure 1   Road freight transport and a privatising economy

116

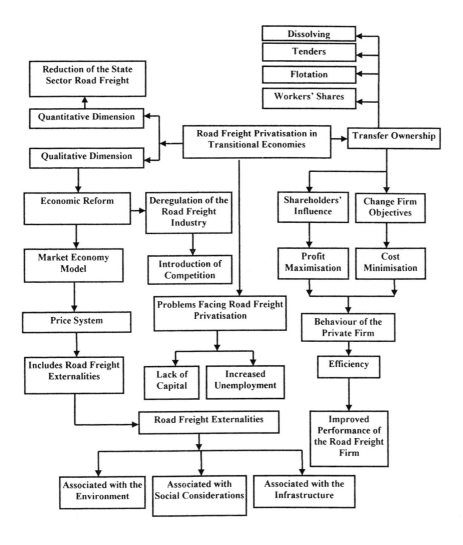

Appendix Figure 2   **The research issues and assumptions**

First round of the Delphi study

The list of 30 statements presented earlier was used to formulate the first round Delphi questionnaire.

The choice of the panel members is crucial in a Delphi exercise. Since participants in the Delphi exercise 'must have a deep interest in the problem and experience to share' (Delbecq, 1975, p.88), it was decided that the panel should include the major parties concerned with privatisation of the road freight industry, who are academics, operators, and government officials. The review of the road freight industry in Egypt has shown that the road freight market comprises the state sector, co-operatives, and private sector operators. The Egyptian panel included the 23 members shown in Appendix Table 1.

Appendix Table 1
Delphi technique - structure and size of the panels

Categories	Egypt	
	Number	%
Academics	6	26.0
Operators	10	43.6
Governmental Officials	7	30.4
Total	**23**	**100**

The first round of the exercise, in Egypt, was mailed in early December 1994, and the first round responses were subsequently analysed. In order to determine whether consensus has been achieved or not, the average percent of majority opinions was used to determine whether the response supports the statements or not. Appendix Table 2 shows the calculation of the average percent of majority opinions. Appendix Figure 3 shows the process of the first round analysis and the formulation of the second round questionnaire.

Appendix Table 2
Delphi technique - first round, average percentage of majority opinions

	Number
Majority agreements	407
Majority disagreements	105
Total opinion expressed	654
Average % of majority opinions *	78.3 %

*Average % of majority opinions =

Majority agreement + majority disagreement / total opinions expressed × 100

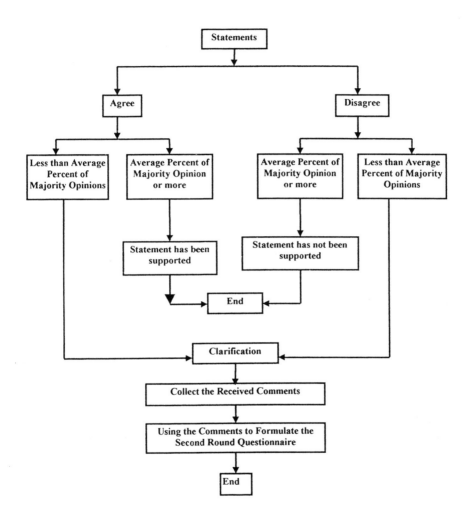

Appendix Figure 3   Delphi technique - first round analysis and
formulation of the second round questionnaire

Results of the first round

Relevant details of the study are included in the main text. Appendix Table 3 shows a summary of the degree of consensus at the end of the first round of the Delphi study.

Appendix Table 3
Delphi technique first round - degree of consensus for the issues

Issues	Agree	Disagree	Total
Impact of privatisation on the road freight industry	166 73.5%	60 26.5%	226
Role of freight management under privatisation	37 80.4%	9 19.6%	46
Best method of achieving privatisation	69 53.1%	61 46.9%	130
Macroeconomic problems facing privatisation	120 69.8%	52 30.2%	172
The external cost of road freight under privatisation	55 69.6%	24 30.4%	79

N.B.: The numbers in the table refer to the number of votes. They vary within the issues according to the number of statements asked in that category.

A lower degree of consensus for an issue category means less certainty and more debate about this issue category, and a higher degree of consensus means the reverse. Among these five conceptual categories (or issues of privatisation), the lowest degree of consensus related to the best method of achieving privatisation, and the highest degree of consensus related to role of freight management under privatisation.

A possible explanation is that the issue of *best method of achieving privatisation* is a more open issue than the others, and is closely linked to other problems facing economies in transition. These are, in particular, the problems of increased unemployment and availability of capital needed for privatisation of the road freight industry. On the other hand, there is probably less doubt and therefore less debate about the *role of freight management under privatisation*. Possibly the experience of other countries, such as the UK, has shown a clear positive impact of privatisation on the road freight industry, but the method of privatising the road freight industry in those countries is not necessary applicable for Egypt. Using the degree of consensus as a base for ranking these five issues, the issue of *best method of achieving privatisation* comes last. Appendix Table 4 shows the rank order of these categories at the end of the first Delphi round.

Appendix Table 4
Delphi technique first round -
ranking of the issues according to degree of consensus

Issues	Rank
Impact of privatisation on the road freight industry	2
Role of freight management under privatisation	1
Best method of achieving privatisation of the road freight industry	5
Macroeconomic problems facing privatisation of the road freight industry	3
The external cost of road freight under privatisation	4

The role of freight management under privatisation and the impact of privatisation on the road freight industry are the clearest issues, followed by macroeconomic problems facing privatisation of the road freight industry.

Second round of Delphi

The second round survey aimed to re-test those statements without a majority opinion in the first round survey, by clarifying the reasons for disagreement, provided by the panellists in the first round survey. Thus, the second round questionnaire included the original statements, each of them followed by a number of sub-statements. These were the comments received from the panellists in the first round as a reason for disagreement with the original statements. The panellists then were asked to re-consider both the original statements and the sub-statements, and supply opinions regarding these sub-statements. The second round of the survey took place in Egypt between May and July 1995, and all 23 experts continued to participate. The replies were analysed using the average percent of majority opinion as applied for the first round in the sequence shown in Appendix Figure 4.

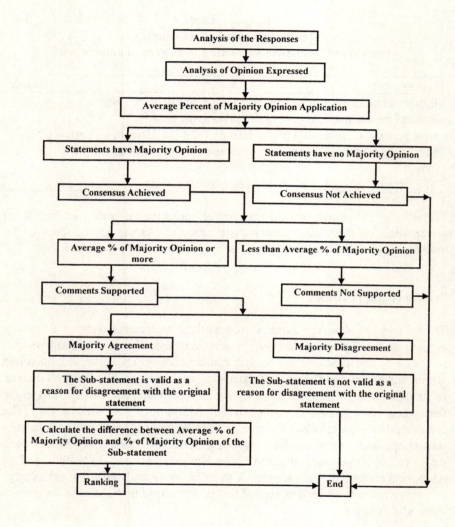

Appendix Figure 4   Delphi technique second round analysis

The following list shows the extent of consensus following the second Delphi round. Again, it is divided according to the five main issues.

Issue 1

Impact of privatisation on the road freight industry.

Statement	*Degree of consensus*
Privatisation will inevitably create a more efficient, flexible and dynamic road freight industry.	*Agree*
Competition is the most important element for a high quality road freight industry.	*Agree*
Under the privatisation of road haulage, the size of the state sector should be minimised as much as possible.	*Agree*
By privatising the road freight industry, there will be an opportunity to release more governmental money for spending on transport infrastructure (especially roads).	*The statement is not valid, because:* • *it depends on the government approach to public spending;* • *no one can be sure about it.*
Road freight customers will benefit from privatising the industry in terms of a better quality of service.	*Agree*
Road freight customers will benefit from privatising the industry in terms of lower charges.	*Agree*
Negative results might result from excessive competition in the transport sector. Therefore, a form of regulation of competition should applied by the government to save the operators' profitability.	*No consensus*

It is not necessary to regulate competition in road freight through the government, because the freight operators can do it voluntarily through self-regulation.

Disagree

A privatised, deregulated road haulage industry requires a legal distinction to be made by the government between own account operators and professional operators.

Agree

Privatisation should not mean withdrawing the subsidies totally from the transport industry. Some parts of the transport system need to be supported.

The statement is not valid, because:
• the subsidies have negative results on the performance;
• there should be subsidies only in the case of passenger transport, to support some social categories and/or achieve some targets, e.g. provide services to remote areas.

Issue 2

Role of freight management under privatisation.

Statement	*Degree of consensus*
To maximise profits should be the main objective for road freight management under privatisation.	*The statement is not valid, because the main target for the management should be to improve the services and reduce cost, then maximising profit could be achieved.*
Under privatisation, identifying areas where cost reduction could be made is the main task for road freight management.	*Agree*

Issue 3

Best method of achieving privatisation of the road freight industry.

Statement	*Degree of consensus*
A good way to achieve privatisation of the road haulage industry is to dissolve the existing companies and sell off all their assets.	*Disagree*
A good way to achieve privatisation of the road haulage industry is to sell off the companies, in their existing form, through tenders.	*Agree*
A good way to achieve privatisation of the road haulage industry is to transfer the companies' assets to shares, which could be sold through the stock exchange.	*The statement is not valid, because:* • *it depends on the financial and technical situation of the company;* • *it could be a good way to privatise the industry, but it first requires financial restructuring for the companies.*
A good way to achieve privatisation of the road haulage industry is to transfer the companies' assets to shares, using part of these shares to encourage early and voluntary retirement of the employees and use the remaining shares as workers' shares.	*The statement is not valid, because:* • *it could be a way to privatise the industry, but it is not the best way;* • *there should be a solution for all the companies' debt problems first, and then the assets should be transferred.*
Different state sector road haulage companies require different forms of privatisation (e.g. privatising management only or privatising both management and ownership).	*Agree*
A wider base of popular capitalism is an important element to achieve successful privatisation of the road haulage industry, and requires low priced shares.	*Agree*

Issue 4

Macroeconomic problems facing privatisation of the road freight industry.

Statement	*Degree of consensus*
The lack of available capital is one of the most important problems facing the privatisation process of the road freight industry in the developing countries.	*The statement is not valid, because:* *• companies' debts and unavailability of data about these companies are the most important problems;* *• total savings in banks is more than the estimated value of these companies, but the people trust bank savings more than investment in companies' shares;* *• there is no shortage of local savings and capital.*
The problem of the lack of available capital could be avoided by allowing foreign capital to buy the assets of the state sector (particularly road haulage).	*The statement is not valid, because:* *• the investment law, passed in 1989, already allows foreign capital to invest in Egypt;* *• there is no shortage of local savings and capital;* *• it could be better if it comes in the form of joint venture companies;* *• road freight sector is a strategic sector, so the foreign capital shares in the company should be less than 50 per cent to avoid foreign capital control.*
Foreign control over the road freight industry will result if foreign capital is allowed to buy state assets in the road freight industry.	*Agree*
The problem of foreign capital control over the road freight industry could be avoided by determining a maximum percentage for the capital owned by a foreigner in the road haulage companies.	*The statement is not valid, because:* *• the ownership should be free to anyone. There is a law and regulations to avoid foreign capital control over the national economy, not only the road freight industry.*

126

	• *the investment law already determines this percentage.*
To avoid the problem of foreign capital control over the road freight industry, the government should sell the shares of the state-owned road haulage companies to their existing employees with interest free credit.	*Agree*
Increased unemployment is one of the most important problems to face the privatisation of the road freight industry.	*Agree*
The ability of the government to pay for dismissed employees (as a result of privatisation), or re-training them, or transferring them to other activities is one of the problems facing the privatisation processes.	*Agree*
The problem of increased unemployment could be overcome by employing revenue from selling state sector road haulage companies to encourage new small road haulage businesses.	*The statement is not valid, because it does not have to be small road haulage businesses.*

Issue 5

The external cost of road freight under privatisation.

Statement	*Degree of consensus*
Under privatisation, road freight operators should pay for the damage to the environment resulting from running their operations.	*The statement is not valid, because as a principle it is acceptable, but the application should be gradually.*
A tax on fuel is adequate to cover the social and environmental costs resulting from road freight operations.	*The statement is not valid, because:* • *it depends on the amount of this tax and whether it covers the cost or not;*

• some research is needed to determine the cost of damage to the environment caused by lorries. External taxes might be needed.

Making private road haulage pay for social and environment costs will result in price increases in the short term.

Agree

In the medium and long terms, cost increases, resulting from private road haulage paying for social and environment costs, will be absorbed by the industry and prices will not be too high.

The statement is not valid, because:
• any increase in the operational cost, will result directly in price increases;
• it could be on the long term, when the number of firms is increased and competition works at its best, but even in the medium term the prices will be too high.

The revised assumptions

The results of the survey are used to revise the assumptions presented earlier in this chapter. The assumptions are reviewed in the light of the panellists' opinions and the results of the two rounds, and new assumptions are formulated, which are presented under the five main issues of privatisation of the road freight industry introduced earlier in this work.

Issue 1

Impact of privatisation on the road freight industry.

Revised assumption 1.1 The productivity of the state sector enterprises is lower than that of the private sector, and privatisation leads to improved performance through the ability to transfer ownership. Therefore, under privatisation of the road freight industry, the size of the state sector should be minimised as much as possible, and subsidies should be withdrawn. Only passenger transport needs to be supported for some social categories and/or achieve some targets, e.g. provide services to remote areas.

Revised assumption 1.2 The effect of privatisation, as a means of increasing efficiency, depends on the introduction of competition, which could be introduced by deregulation. Road freight customers will benefit from privatising the industry in terms of a better quality of service at lower charges.

Revised assumption 1.3 Deregulation may result in excessive competition. To regulate competition by the government and/or through self-regulation may also have negative results, where competition should be free. A legal distinction between own account operators and professional operators, and price guidelines may eliminate the negative results of excessive competition.

Issue 2

Role of freight management under privatisation.

Revised assumption 2.1 The transfer to private ownership will result in improved cost efficiency by sharpening managerial incentives. Although privatisation may entail the adoption of management objectives that respond to the wishes of the shareholders, which is maximising profits, the main target for freight management under privatisation should be to improve quality of service.

Issue 3

Best method of achieving privatisation of the road freight industry.

Revised assumption 3.1 The privatisation of the state sector road freight companies presents different options. Different state sector road haulage companies require different forms of privatisation. Dissolving the companies and selling off their assets is not one of the desirable approaches, where it presents a loss of the national wealth. To put companies' shares in the stock exchange, selling the companies through tenders, and employee buy-outs are preferable.

Issue 4

The external cost of road freight under privatisation.

Revised assumption 4.1 When applying the market economy model and price system, the operators should pay for the externalities. It will result in price increases, but in the long term, when the number of firms is increased and competition works at its best, and through cost reductions, any cost increase would be absorbed by the industry, and as a result the price will not be too high.

Issue 5

Macroeconomic problems facing privatisation of the road freight industry.

Original assumption 5.1 The problem of required capital to finance privatisation, due to the lack of domestic savings, could be overcome by allowing foreign capital to participate in the privatisation process. The fear of foreign control over industries could be overcome by determining the maximum percentage of foreign capital in the companies, or by using employee buy-outs.

The original assumption 5.1 is not revised.

Revised assumption 5.2 The problem of increased unemployment arises from the fact that the economies in transition operate with excess demand for labour, due to the type of technology used and to achieve the social objective of full employment of the work force. On the other hand, the government ability to pay for the dismissed employees, or re-training them, or transferring them to other sectors is limited. The revenue from privatisation could be employed to create new opportunities. Therefore, there is no significant change to assumption 5.2.

References

Delbecq, A.L., Van de Ven, A.H. and Gustafson, D.H. (1975), *Group Techniques for Program Planning*, Scott, Foresman, Glenview: Ill.

Linstone, H. and Turoff, M. (1975) (eds.), *The Delphi Method: Techniques and Applications*, Addison-Wesley: London.